THE ISLANDS SERIES

CRETE

THE ISLANDS SERIES

Achill
The Åland Islands
Alderney
The Aran Islands
The Isle of Arran
The Island of Bute
Canary Islands: Fuerteventura
Cape Breton Island
Corsica
Cyprus
*Dominica
The Falkland Islands

Gotland
Grand Bahama

Harris and Lewis
The Isle of Mull
Jamaica
Jersey
Lundy
The Maltese Islands
Mauritius
*Minorca
Orkney
*Puerto Rico
Rhodes
The Ryukyu Islands

St Kilda and Other Hebridean Islands
*Sardinia
The Isles of Scilly
*The Seychelles
Shetland
*Sicily
*Singapore
Skye
*The Solomon Islands
Staffa
Tasmania
Uist and Barra
Vancouver Island

in preparation

Colonsay and Oronsay
Fiji
Guadeloupe
Guernsey
The Holy Island of Lindisfarne
The Six Inner Hebrides
Islay
Sark
Tahiti
Tobago
Tonga
Valentia

---

* Published in the United States by Stackpole
All other titles published in the United States by David & Charles Inc
The series is distributed in Australia by Wren Publishing Pty Ltd, Melbourne

CRETE

*by ELIZABETH CLUTTON AND
ANDRÉ KENNY*

DAVID & CHARLES

WTON ABBOT LONDON NORTH POMFRET (VT) VANCOUVER

ISBN 0 7153 6789 7
Library of Congress Catalog Card Number 75-26 362

© Elizabeth Clutton and André Kenny 1976

All rights reserved. No part of this publication may be reproduced, stored in a retrieval system, or transmitted, in any form or by any means, electronic, mechanical, photocopying, recording or otherwise, without the prior permission of David & Charles (Holdings) Limited

Set in 11 on 13pt Monotype Baskerville
and printed in Great Britain
by Latimer Trend & Company Ltd Plymouth
for David & Charles (Holdings) Limited
South Devon House Newton Abbot Devon

Published in the United States of America
by David & Charles Inc
North Pomfret Vermont 05053 USA

Published in Canada
by Douglas David & Charles Limited
132 Philip Avenue North Vancouver BC

CONTENTS

		page
	Acknowledgements	6
	Illustrations	7
	Note on Foreign Words and Place-names	9
1	Approach to Crete	11
2	Topography and Geology	19
3	Climate, Vegetation and Land Use	41
4	Communications and Transport	56
5	Prehistory	67
6	Crete under the Romans, the Arabs and Byzantium	92
7	Crete under the Venetians	98
8	Crete since the Seventeenth Century	118
9	Rural Life, Traditional and Modern	144
10	The Towns and Urban Life	165
11	Services and Administration	188
	Appendix: The Offshore Islands	195
	Bibliography	198
	Index	203

ACKNOWLEDGEMENTS

ONE special debt must first be acknowledged, that which we both owe to the late R. W. Hutchinson: he was a gentle, learned man and a generous friend. While writing this book about an island which he knew and loved so well, we have felt his loss and sorely missed his scholarship and humanity.

During the years, we have made many friends in Crete and we are grateful to them all for their friendship and hospitality, for their practical help and encouragement, and for sharing with us their island. Special thanks go to Manoli Chalkiadakis, Eleni and Nikos Kornilakis, Manoussos Manoussakis, and John and Joanna Mavrommatis; also to Chris Kosseris, Constantine Koniatakis, Stergios Spanakis, Aristidis Kriaris, Petros Petrakis, the Houmerianos brothers, Mr Michaeloudakis and Mr Papageorgiou.

Our tentative first drafts were much improved as a result of helpful comments from many friends, in particular Dorothea Gray of St Hugh's College, Oxford; Jennifer Bray of the University of Hong Kong; Mrs Margaret Lewis of Sheffield, and Margaret Wilkes, Map Curator of the National Library of Scotland. We are grateful to Mrs Ann Barham of the Department of Geography, University of Sheffield, for her expert help with the Bibliography, and to Sheila Clark for typing the bulk of the manuscript.

Credit for the illustrations is due largely to much hard work by the cartographers and photographic technicians of the Department of Geography, University of Sheffield. Our thanks are due to them all, but particularly to Jack Hall for the excellent line drawings and for many of the maps, and to Peter Morley for overseeing the photographic work.

Photographs are reproduced by courtesy of J. Allan Cash Ltd, except those marked with an asterisk, which are supplied by the authors, and those marked with a dagger, which are by courtesy of the National Tourist Organisation of Greece.

ILLUSTRATIONS

PLATES	page
Dry farming of cereals and olives near Gournia	33
*Aerial view of Khania	34
Messara Plain	34
Ayia Triadha: the site of the Minoan palace	51
†Phaistos: part of the Minoan site	51
The fourth-century church of St Titus	52
Panormos church	52
The countryside around the ruins of Knossos	69
*Knossos: the Palace of Minos	70
A row of storage jars at the Palace of Minos	70
†Iraklion: Venetian fort and inner harbour	87
†The Morosini fountain in the old town centre	87
†View of Iraklion, showing the old and new harbours	88
†A street market	88
Mires: the bus station	121
†Men relaxing in a local café	122
Mires: a street scene	122
A vineyard in central Crete	139
Sultana grapes being packed for transport	139
Panormos: a cooper at work	140
Panormos: wine barrels lined up in the yard	140
†Peasant woman riding to work on a donkey	157

CRETE

	page
*Animal-powered chain pump	158
†Woman of Anoghia selling handwoven rugs	158
†Ayios Nikolaos: part of the town	175
†Village street in Anoyia	175
†Fishermen repairing their nets	176
†Ayios Nikolaos: the harbour	176

IN TEXT

Polythene greenhouses	55
Knossos: a conjectural reconstruction of the Palace at Minos	76
Monastery of Arkadhi, exterior	143
Traditional method of threshing	164
Morosini Fountain, Iraklion	187

MAPS

Crete in the centre of the Eastern Mediterranean Basin	13
Nomos of Khania (western Crete)	20
Nomos of Rethymnon (west-central Crete)	27
Nomos of Iraklion (east-central Crete)	30
Nomos of Lassithi (eastern Crete)	36
Vegetation of Crete	46
Road network of Crete, 1948 and 1967	62
Main archaeological sites	73
The eastern Mediterranean after the 4th Crusade, c 1220 AD	107
Iraklion: old city and modern suburbs	168
Khania: street plan of the central area	179

NOTE ON FOREIGN WORDS
AND PLACE-NAMES

THE authors' concern has been to render foreign, and especially Greek, names and words in a way that will preserve the familiarity of those which are well known to the English reader and will reflect the pronunciation of those which may not be known to him at all. We have chosen not to adopt any of the conventional systems for the transliteration of Greek place-names and other Greek words, but have preferred instead a commonsense approach in which intelligibility has been put before ritual consistency. Thus, the Greek letter PHI (φ) has usually been transliterated 'ph', as in Phaestos, but has occasionally been rendered 'f' where this seems to give a more familiar and less forbidding word. The Greek letter BETA (β) is in its Greek pronunciation closer to an English 'v' sound and is written as such, the English letter 'b' being used to render its Greek equivalent 'mp', as in Τομπρούκ—literally 'Tomprouk' but more familiar as Tobruk. We have retained the double 's' in Knossos, Tylissos, Amnissos and similar names.

Classical Greek and Latin authors whose names have become in their anglicised form part of the English language are called by their English names—Strabo, not Strabon; Homer, not Omiros. Similarly, the title of this book is *Crete*, not Kriti, and we write of Athens, not Athinai. We have used the Greek names for places called after Christian saints—eg Ayia Varvára and Ayios Nikólaos, not St Barbara and St Nicholas. Iráklion, now the administrative capital of Crete, is called by this name throughout the book. This prevents any confusion arising from

CRETE

the use of the city's Venetian name 'Candia', used until recently not only for the city but also for the island as a whole. It also avoids possible confusion with Canea, the old capital in the west, referred to throughout by its modern name of Khaniá.

As an aid to the correct pronunciation of unfamiliar Greek words and place-names, an accent has been added—at first mention only—to indicate the stressed syllable.

Exceptions to these general principles occur only where we have quoted from works by other authors.

1 APPROACH TO CRETE

WITH so much surviving from the past and so much that is modern, Crete today is an intriguing mixture of old and new, not only in its landscape and buildings, but in the activities and attitudes of its people. To travel in Crete is to travel through time in a random and ever-changing order. The visitor is provided with a continuous pageant of contrasts from the relentless rhythm of the *bouzouki* blaring from a café jukebox, to the timeless serenity of a saint held motionless in a Byzantine fresco; from the efficient anonymity of a modern international air terminal to the picturesque inconvenience of a medieval city. The more prosperous young men race about the streets on bright, noisy Japanese motor cycles, frightening old women on foot, swathed in dusty black, and the menfolk on their donkeys, sitting across the great wooden pack-saddles.

Numerous social customs recall the centuries of Turkish occupation: these include the long little finger-nail on the right hand, worn to demonstrate that its owner is above manual work; the presence of men, and only men, in certain cafés, sometimes smoking the *narghilé* (hookah); and the wearing by a few older men of the traditional dark baggy trousers and high Cretan boots. Some of the younger men have adopted a more modern and streamlined dress, retaining the knee-length leather boots and wearing them with tailored breeches.

In the cities, buildings of many styles and periods provide a varied backdrop to the bustle of human activity. Modern hotels and flats, large dilapidated Turkish houses with wooden shutters, balconies and high-ceilinged, airy rooms, back up against massive city walls emblazoned with the winged Lion of St Mark, symbol in Crete of the Venetian occupation. Street names commemorate heroes of Greek mythology, fighters against the Turks, great soldiers and statesmen, and martyrs in recent wars.

In the countryside, the progression of the seasons sets the pace and rhythm of life, and controls its activities. Shortly after dawn the daily procession from the village to the fields takes place, returning at sunset. The farmer may travel on foot, on a donkey, in his own van or three-wheeler, or by bus. During his work in the fields he may use modern irrigation pumps and tractors, or hand sickles for harvesting and wooden threshing tools indistinguishable from those described by Roman writers of the first century BC.

Standing high above the coastal cities and the hillside vineyards and olive groves are the great mountains of Crete. From whatever quarter the traveller approaches, it is the mountains that dominate his first impressions. In summer they are misty in outline and grey in eminence, but tawny and arid when seen from close quarters; in winter, clear-cut, shining bright with snow. Today a place of peace and solitude, in the past they were a refuge from tyranny. Only in times of direst trouble have the Cretans fled to the high treeless plateaux and exposed mountain slopes to live in caves and crudely built stone shelters. On almost every point of vantage are rough walls that tell of desperate defence, with grim and merciless slaughter for its end.

The Cretan pride which held itself upright against long centuries of foreign rule is to be seen still in the personal demeanour of individual Cretans and in their fierce love of their own land, whether it be their farm, their town or Crete itself. It is this above all else that makes Crete truly what they call it: the 'Great Island'.

THE LOCATION OF CRETE

No longer the cultural centre of the world, and no longer a remote and neglected colony on the periphery of a vast and decaying empire, Crete today is the southernmost region of Greece, to which it was united in 1913. By air, it is four and a

APPROACH TO CRETE

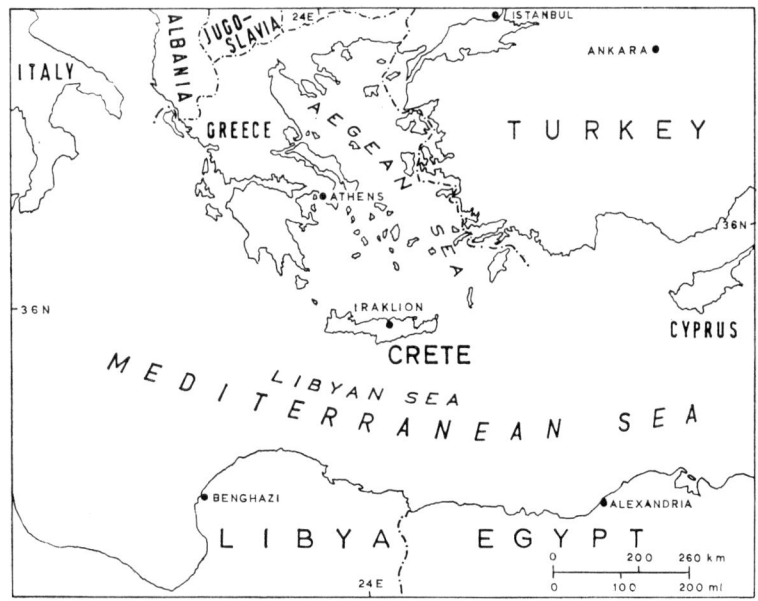

Crete in the centre of the Eastern Mediterranean Basin

half hours from London, and forty-five minutes from Athens; by sea, it is at the end of an overnight journey from Piraeus.

The island of Crete lies almost in the centre of the eastern Mediterranean basin, south-east of the mainland of Greece. It is situated between 34° 55′ and 35° 41′ N, and 23° 30′ and 26° 19′ E. In shape it resembles a narrow rectangle 256 kilometres (159 miles) long from west to east, and varying in width between 57 kilometres at its widest and 12 kilometres at its narrowest. Its area is about 8,280 square kilometres (3,200 square miles).

SEA ROUTES

The configuration of the island, which has four of its five best harbours and all its main towns in the north, has concentrated external maritime traffic on that coast. The shortest distance between the mainland of Greece and Crete is about

CRETE

100 kilometres, from the southern capes of the Peloponnese to Cape Graboúsa, the north-western tip of Crete. When the Venetians controlled Crete this was their easiest route to the island; it had the advantage also that the small islands of Kýthera and Antikythera were available *en route* for refuge in case of bad weather. If weather conditions were favourable, the Venetians reckoned that a month was needed for the voyage from Venice to Crete via the Adriatic and the coast of the Peloponnese.

When the Turks had conquered Crete and deprived the Venetians of their trade with the East, communications between Crete and the Christian countries of Europe virtually ceased. The chief routes for passengers from Europe to Crete, throughout the period from the mid-seventeenth century to the end of the nineteenth, were indirect and lay via Syria, Smyrna or Constantinople.

In 1845 the French traveller Victor Raulin set off from Paris at the start of a journey to Crete. He spent more than six months on the island, investigating its geography and natural history, and returned home in 1846. The outward and inward routes and timetables of his journey give a fascinating insight into the uncertainties of long-distance Mediterranean travel in the last century. Raulin left Paris on 4 April 1845 and stayed three days at Marseilles, leaving on 11 April in the steamship *Eurotas*. The first port of call was the great Aegean port of Syra, which was reached on the 22nd. The *Eurotas* then went on to Smyrna, but Raulin remained on Syra waiting for a passage to Crete. He left on a Greek sailing ship, probably a caïque, on 1 May and had his first sight of the mountains of Crete early the next morning. To his great frustration, the vessel was then becalmed offshore and did not finally arrive at Khaniá until 3 May.

On 17 December 1845 Raulin began his return journey to Paris aboard 'the little steamer *Kirit* which the Pasha had had built in England in order to establish a regular service [from Khania] to Syra and Smyrna. The crew were all English, except for the purser, who was a Mussulman'. The vessel berthed at Syra the next morning, and later that day left by

APPROACH TO CRETE

way of Chios for Smyrna, arriving there on the 21st. Raulin could not obtain an onward passage until 27 December, when he embarked on the *Ferdinando Primo*, reaching Constantinople on the 29th. After a further delay lasting until 7 January, he took passage for Marseilles on *Le Tancréde*. The first call was at the Piraeus on 10 January and the second at Valetta on 13 January. The ship did not leave Malta until almost a fortnight later, proceeding via Naples to Marseilles, where she arrived on 2 February, having been delayed by the *mistral*. The customs formalities were not completed until the next day. Even then Raulin's delays were not ended—he did not reach Paris until 15 February 1846. This adds up to thirty days from Paris to Khania via Marseilles and Syra, and sixty days for the return journey via Constantinople and Malta. On the outward journey the actual sailing time from Marseilles to Khania was eleven days to Syra, plus two days from Syra to Crete, thirteen days in all, counting one night in a calm. On the return, the total was thirty-two days.

Before the liberation of Greece in 1833, the island port of Syra had the largest freight and passenger traffic of any harbour in Greece. After the liberation, when Athens became the capital, the adjacent port of the Piraeus grew in importance, and direct sea links were established with Crete. The passenger traffic to and from the Greek mainland was carried by ships which ran from the Piraeus to either Iráklion or Khania; those sailing direct to Iraklion then went on to Réthymnon and Khania, and vice versa. Each vessel thus called at all three of the main north coast ports, and this practice continued until the mid-1960s.

Before World War II when port facilities were very limited, larger ships were unable to enter the harbour at Iraklion and small boats ferried ashore both passengers and freight. The same thing happened at Rethymnon and Khania and, since none of the three was accessible in bad weather, passengers had to keep in close touch with the ship's agent in order to find out whether they had to take a bus to one of the other ports where conditions might be better. The bus was available after about

1920, but before that one merely waited for the next boat. Indeed, it was often more prudent to wait since, in a rough sea, it could take two days to make the Piraeus from Crete.

Khania had a slight advantage over the other two ports for, if the weather was too bad for rowing boats from the Venetian harbour to reach a steamer standing offshore, the ship could be transferred to Soúdha Bay where she could safely lie at anchor until the boats could get to her. During the winter, in fact, this was the normal procedure; at other times the ship would signal to the telegraph station at the entrance to Soudha Bay if she were not going to Khania. Word would then be sent to the ship's agent and to the taxi drivers of Khania to go the rounds of the cafés and warn intending passengers to drink up. In very bad weather, many captains on leaving the shelter of Soudha Bay would not run straight for the mouth of the Saronic Gulf, but would take the old route of the galleys and sailing ships via Kythera and Antikythera to Cape Malea before turning again past Spetsai and Ydhra to make their way to Piraeus by a less windy course. Speed was not the object; rather it was to arrive and to show the owners how little fuel had been used.

The journey now is very different: overnight car ferries run direct from the Piraeus to Iraklion and to Soudha. The journey takes about thirteen hours, and there are drive-on/drive-off facilities at each end. For cheapness, speed and comfort the ships working this crossing compare favourably with any vessel on the Channel service between England and France. In Soudha Bay, Crete possesses the finest sheltered harbour in the Mediterranean basin, with deep-water berths alongside its civil and naval quays. At Iraklion, the new harbour is crowded throughout the spring, summer and autumn months with holiday cruise liners. Efforts to improve the harbour at Rethymnon have not met with success and no regular ferry service now visits the port. An inter-island passenger service still plies between the large new concrete mole at Ayios Nikolaos, the tiny port of Sitía, Rhodes, the Piraeus and Thíra. This service is worked weekly in each direction and is the only surviving small boat service to

APPROACH TO CRETE

link Crete directly with the other islands of Greece. There are no regular services running beyond Crete from any of its south coast ports and harbours.

AIR ROUTES

The first passengers to fly to Crete on a regular air service were carried on a Short 'Calcutta' flying boat of Imperial Airways Ltd on 30 March 1929. The island was a stage on the flight to India, and neatly divided the passage from Athens (Megálo Pefko) to Alexandria. At first the aircraft called at the naval flying-boat base at Soudha but, by 1 May 1931, when the Short 'Kent' (Scipio) flying boats were introduced to the Mediterranean, Imperial Airways had their own landing area in Eloúnda Bay, just north of Ayios Nikolaos. Under the name of Mirabella, this remained the main international air base of Crete for several years. There were few facilities: a launch for the passengers and freight, a floating bowser or two, a yacht to accommodate the resident staff, and a generating plant for the flare-path. Of the few passengers who stayed in Crete, almost all were archaeologists on their way to Knossós; they preferred the comfort and glamour of the flying boats to the relative squalor of the steamboat passage. The service, then run by the 'C' class boats, finally ceased on 11 June 1940 after the capitulation of France to the Germans.

After the last flying boat had left, the bowsers and the boats departed and for long years no international air route came to Crete. Greek domestic airlines began to serve the island as soon as the airports were opened to them after World War II. Iraklion had its airport by the coast to the east, but Khania had to depend on the old fighter air strip at Maléme until the international airport on Akrotíri was opened. Khania now has a daily service from Athens, but the growth point for air traffic in Crete is the prestigious new international airport at Iraklion. This was brought up to international standard by enlarging existing runways and erecting a new terminal building and

CRETE

control tower. The airport is well sited some 4 kilometres east of the town, adjacent to the new National Road linking the main cities of Crete. The new facilities were built without interrupting air traffic to the old airport, and were officially opened for flying on 1 January 1970, some months before the new control tower was completed. The main runway lies parallel to the seashore and will accommodate any civil aircraft likely to be operating in the area. It has even been suggested that if supersonic aircraft are excluded from Athens (Ellinikó) airport, Iraklion may become the chief international airport in Greece.

2 TOPOGRAPHY AND GEOLOGY

MOST travellers have their first sight of the island at dawn, as their ship approaches Iraklion. As the sky lightens, the first grey outline acquires colour and detail. The long low arms of the harbour reveal themselves, with the solitary peak of Iúktas in the background and, to the west, the high cliffs where Mt Ídha comes down to the sea, and the white houses of Rogdhiá cling to the steep rock. If the morning is clear, the traveller will see behind the coastal plain and above the low hills of Knossos some of the high mountains of Crete, extending east and west in an almost unbroken spine throughout the length of the island.

These mountains, which give Crete its special character, are the remains of a once-continuous arc of folds which stretched from the Peloponnese through Crete to Asia Minor. Tertiary in origin, this arc itself forms a small part of a much larger system of Alpine mountain-building which created a long chain of mountains from the Pyrenees in the west, through the Swiss and Austrian Alps and the Dinaric Alps of Jugoslavia, down through Greece and Crete to the Taurus Mountains in the east. Subsequent fractures and subsidences have broken up parts of the arc and Crete has become an isolated mountain mass on the southern fringe of the Aegean Sea. Faulting and movement within the island itself, followed by erosion and in some places by marine deposition, have led to the separating out of the main mountain masses and thus to the formation of a number of physically distinct regions. Each region, mountain or lowland, has its particular features of topography and its particular points of interest.

CRETE

WESTERN CRETE

This part of Crete includes the two principal mountain massifs, the Lefká Óri (the White Mountains) and Psilorítis (Mt Idha), together with the hilly areas which separate them and which lie to the west of the White Mountains. Geologically, this is the most varied part of the island.

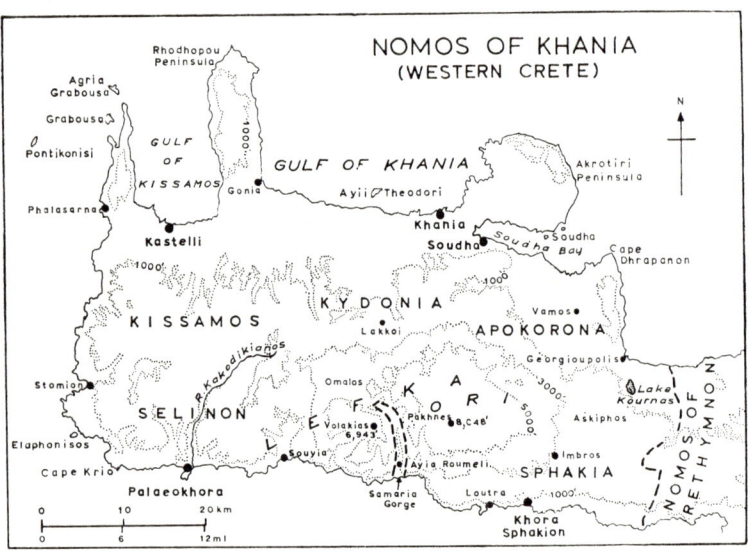

Sélinon, Kíssamos and the West Coast

This is the only area of Crete where large stretches of the basement rocks underlying the Tertiary folds can be seen. These are mostly highly folded, metamorphosed Triassic rocks which occur as phyllites, mica-schists, slates and quartzites. Among the few impervious rocks in the island, their occurrence in the two western Eparchies (administrative districts) of Kissamos and Selinon, has resulted in what is for Crete an unusually gentle topography, characterised by rounded hills and valleys. Only

TOPOGRAPHY AND GEOLOGY

in the occasional river gorges and on the coasts, where limestone appears, does the landscape become harsh and forbidding. The full length of the western coast, from Cape Grabousa in the north to Cape Krío (The Ram) in the south, is steep and rocky.

At the southern end of the promontory of Grabousa is the ancient site of Phalásarna. The floor of the harbour of the old city is now about 8 metres (26ft) above sea level and at the foot of the ancient quays the harbour bed is ploughed and sown with grain. Other evidence from western Crete—for example, the raised beaches at Goniá—suggests the general uplifting of this part of the island by a similar amount. In the eastern half of the island there has been a corresponding sinking, with the result that parts of some ancient sites are now below sea level. Mókhlos, for example, now a small island lying off the north coast, was once a peninsula joined by a causeway to the mainland (see Appendix B).

South of Phalasarna, the coast continues in a series of cliffs, broken occasionally by sandy or rocky beaches. Twenty-five kilometres further on, the road from Kastélli Kissámou on the north coast descends a valley via Mýli, Élos and Perivólia to the coast at Stómion. Nearby, the monastery of Khrysoskalítissa (St Mary of the Golden Staircase), with its solitary date-palm, stands on a knob of rock overlooking the sea. Southwards from the monastery the shoreline presents a uniformly inhospitable front, with stretches of rocky raised beach backed by cliffs, giving way to cliffs at the water's edge beyond Cape Krio (Strabo's Kriou Metopon). The town of Palaeokhóra is 9 kilometres east of the cape, on a small promontory at the mouth of the valley of the River Kakodikiános, through which the main road leads steeply northwards across the shales and talschists to the north coast.

The North Coast, from Cape Grabousa to Rogdhia

To the north of Selinon and the rounded valleys of Kissamos lie the alluvial plains and hard limestone promontories of the north coast. At the western end of the island two such promontories,

CRETE

Grabousa and Rhodhopóu, project northwards into the Sea of Crete, with the Gulf of Kissamos between them. On the shore of the gulf lies the small town of Kastelli. East of Rhodopou extends the much larger Gulf of Khania, bounded some 30 kilometres to the east by the broad promontory of Akrotiri. The city of Khania, which for nearly 500 years until 1970 was the administrative capital of the island, lies near the eastern angle of the bay. As a port, Khania is less than satisfactory; its Venetian harbour, the Mandráki (Little Sheepfold), can only be used in fair weather. South and west of the city is Crete's second largest alluvial lowland, the plain of Khania. This fertile plain, watered by many springs, is perennially shaded by the deep green of the orange groves and the glaucous tints of the olives.

The peninsula of Akrotiri is approached from Khania via a short isthmus, $4\frac{1}{2}$ kilometres wide. The peninsula itself is 12 kilometres long and 15 kilometres wide. The road from Khania climbs steeply and leads to a plateau some 500 metres (1,640ft) above the sea, with higher mountains at its northern and eastern ends. It is on this plateau that the life of Akrotiri is concentrated, with its villages, its monasteries, its fields and its pastures. On the southern part of the plateau is the State airport of Khania, and on the cliffs to the east is a NATO missile firing base.

To the south of the peninsula is the deep fjord-like inlet of Soudha Bay, with Soudha Island at its entrance and the town of Soudha at its head. The bay is 15 kilometres long from west to east, and 4 kilometres wide, and has a depth of water sufficient for the largest ships. Soudha is the port of Khania, and owes much of its character and prosperity to the existence there of a naval base used by NATO ships. The prospect from the cliffs of Akrotiri, when seen on a clear day in winter, must rival for breadth and grandeur any panorama in Crete. At the observer's feet is the bay of Soudha, in peace a haven but in war a potential trap for ships. Then, below the southern sky, are seen the summits and the silver flanks of the White Mountains. Above the orange groves of Kissamos and Khania, above the heights

TOPOGRAPHY AND GEOLOGY

of Itzedín and the hills of Vámos, eastward, beyond Cape Dhrápanon (The Sickle), beyond the fort and minarets of Rethymnon and the holy bloodstained fortress of Arkádhi, the pure line of white runs on, until it meets the towering crests of Idha.

From Soudha to Rethymnon, some 50 kilometres to the east, the land rises from the coast in a series of fertile hills and valleys until the peaks of the White Mountains are reached. About 3 kilometres inland from the shore of Georgioúpolis Bay, and about 17 kilometres west of Rethymnon is Lake Kournás, the only fresh-water lake in Crete. It is squarish in shape, about $1\frac{1}{2}$ kilometres across, and its depth, when measured in 1949, was 64 metres (210ft). Its normal water level is 20 metres (66ft) above the sea, but it is subject to periodic rises caused by variations, said to take place every five years, in the discharge of the springs which well up in its south-west corner. Inland the lake is enclosed by high hills, which to the west and south rise steeply from its waters. On the north side, where the ground is lower, the surplus water from the lake is led to irrigate the land near the sea. The whole area round the lake gives an impression of gentleness which is absent from the grander landscapes of Crete.

The city of Rethymnon was important as a fortress and a port under the Venetians, and the walls of their castle still stand above the present town. The prosperity of the place has declined with the silting up of the harbour, and a modern attempt to revive sea trade by building a new harbour has been frustrated in the same way. The revolution in the island's transport over the last few years has brought cheese-making down from the mountains into factories in the town, and this trade, along with the growth of tourism, should ensure that Rethymnon will recover at least some of its former prosperity.

An irrigated coastal plain extends eastwards from Rethymnon and is mostly devoted to the culture of peanuts. The plain terminates about 25 kilometres to the east, at which point a low range of mountains cuts across it to the sea. These mountains lie north of the main mountain mass of Psiloritis and are separated from its flanks by the broad green valley of the Mylopótamos (Mill River). One of the largest rivers in Crete and one of the most constant in flow, it rises on the north-eastern slopes of Psiloritis. After flowing for some distance northwards it turns westwards to Pérama, then northwards again, breaking through the range of hills that separates it from the sea. In its westward course, the river has cut a wide, deep valley through the rough limestone hills, and the prosperity of Perama is built upon the fertility of this valley and of the plain of Angelianá north of the town. The high (1,100 metres; 3,609ft) craggy hills between the Mylopotamos valley and the coast end at the sea in cliffs, broken only here and there, as at Phódele, where a small torrent runs into the sea. About 10 kilometres east of Phódele the mountains end suddenly, with an abrupt descent of 1,000 metres (3,281ft) where the cliffs beyond Rogdhia fall away to the low land west of Iraklion.

The Lefka Ori (White Mountains)

Dazzling with snow in winter and with bare white rock in summer, the Lefka Ori dominate the western end of the island. The chief peaks all rise above 2,000 metres (6,562ft), Pákhnes at 2,453 metres (8,048ft) being the highest. The untouchable purity of these mountains, and their inaccessibility, have combined to give them a special significance. To the Cretans they are a shining stronghold, the inviolate nursery and the eternal symbol of their freedom; to the visitor they show some of the finest and most spectacular scenery in the island.

The massif as a whole is the largest single mountain block in Crete. It is formed of hard massive limestones, thousands of metres thick, and its foot-hills rise from the north, west and east in a series of ridges leading up to the summits themselves. High up among these peaks, north of the crest of Volakiás—2,116 metres (6,943ft)—and hidden from below is the polje, or elevated plain, of Omalós. Its flat circular floor, some 5 kilometres in diameter, is covered by alluvium washed from the

TOPOGRAPHY AND GEOLOGY

surrounding heights, and stands 1,140 metres (3,740ft) above sea level. The plain is surrounded by a ring of steep, stony limestone hills rising directly to 500–1,000 metres (1,640–3,281ft) above its floor. No river breaks through these hills, but the plain is drained through a series of peripheral holes, known as *katavóthras* or swallow-holes. These are at the northern end, near where the road from Khania enters over a steep pass. The fertile soil is cultivated in the summer and, when they are clear of snow, the surrounding hills provide pasture. Beyond the southern edge of the plain a narrow valley leads steeply upwards to the abrupt col separating it from a precipitous descent into the gorge of Samária.

This gorge is the longest, deepest and most spectacular in Europe. Its 18-kilometre length offers a path for the strong and agile from its head at Xilóskalo (Wooden Ladder) on the rim of Omalos to the Libyan Sea 1,200 metres (3,937ft) below. The gorge cuts down a full 600 metres (1,969ft) into the heart of the White Mountains; at this depth, at the place known as the Iron Gates, the walls are no more than 3 metres apart. In summer, the boulder-strewn floor of the ravine forms the only path; in winter, there is nothing but a fast-flowing torrent. Here at all seasons is one of the great solitudes of Europe. Half-way along the gorge is the now-deserted village of Samaria, with the fourteenth-century church of St Mary. At the mouth of the great ravine is the tiny village of Ayia Rouméli, separated from Palaeokhora to the westward by 28 kilometres of cliff-bound shore. The only break in the walls of towering limestone is at Soúyia, 16 kilometres west of Ayia Roumeli, where a torrent bed provides a rough track to a few mountain villages.

Eastwards from Ayia Roumeli the character of the coast remains unchanged. Throughout the 18-kilometre stretch which separates Ayia Roumeli from Khóra Sphakión, the tall cliffs are broken only at Cape Móuros. The cape has a sandy bay on either side and on the eastern bay stands the village port of Loutrá, with the islet of Loutra, 12 metres (39ft) high, just offshore. This remote spot is, according to the *Mediterranean*

25

CRETE

Pilot, 'the only bay on the southern side of Kriti where a vessel would be secure in winter'. Unfortunately, however, the hinterland of Loutra consists of bare mountain slopes and there is no practicable way into the interior.

From Loutra it is 6 kilometres to Khora Sphakion (Place of the Sphakiots); this village, which throughout the centuries was the focus of armed resistance to invaders, now consists of a few inhabited houses clustered round the tiny harbour. Pashley (1837) estimated that the pre-1821 population of Khora Sphakion exceeded 12,000. Today, it is only a few hundred, and the ruined homes of former inhabitants surround the present village, their grey walls echoing a turbulent past. Inland a winding gorge carries a motor road northwards through the eastern flanks of the White Mountains. Although in places as narrow as the Gorge of Samaria, the Sphakia gorge is less deep. At about 765 metres (2,510ft) the gorge opens suddenly on to the Plain of Ímbros, above which the road climbs to a col at 807 metres (2,648ft) and then descends into the Plain of Askiphós. The mountain polje is 5–6 kilometres in circumference, its regularity of form being broken towards the north by a rocky island on which there is an ancient fortress. Although covered with snow during the winter, the plain is fertile and in summer vines, cereals and other crops are grown, tended by the inhabitants of the village which lies at the southern edge of the plain.

The Isthmus of Rethymnon and Psiloritis

Eastwards from the ring of mountains surrounding Askiphos, the land falls away towards the isthmus of Rethymnon. The hard Jurassic limestones give place to a mixture of softer, more recent rocks belonging to the marine Upper Tertiary series. Throughout most of the isthmus, marls alternate with early limestones, although sandstones and conglomerates occur locally. The associated topography forms a marked contrast to the hard limestone massifs on either side. The land is much lower and consists of a succession of broad ridges and valleys,

TOPOGRAPHY AND GEOLOGY

irregularly aligned, and covered with stony but mostly cultivable soils. The roads follow winding courses through the valleys, linking the villages and, although the island is relatively narrow in this area, there is no quick route through from the north to the south coasts.

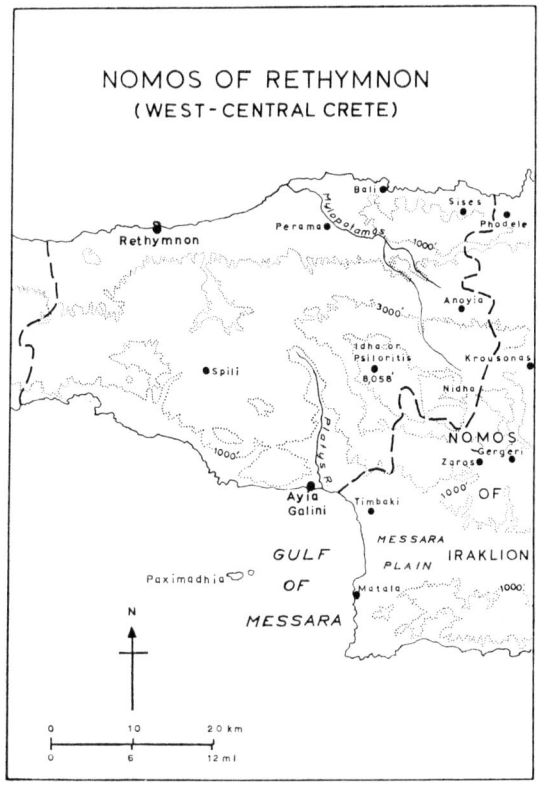

The area as a whole is orientated northwards towards Rethymnon, and has turned its back on the south coast: throughout the entire 55-kilometre stretch of coastline from Khora Sphakion to Ayia Galíni, at the western end of the Messará Plain, there are no main routeways through to the coast, and no ports. The hills and mountains lying immediately behind the coast are barren, and development has remained at a minimum. From Ayia Galini, with its tiny harbour and sandy beach, a long through route leads northwards up the valley of the Plátys river, over the divide into the valley of the Sphakorýako and ultimately to Rethymnon.

Eastwards from this route, and southwards from the main north coast road, the central range of mountains begins to rise slowly at first, then more steeply, ridge on ridge to the twin peaks of Psiloritis (Idha). These are clearly seen from both north and south, and their striking outline, snow-covered except in high summer, remains in the traveller's mind to be sought at each return. The higher of the two peaks is called Tímios Stavrós and is, at 2,456 metres (8,058ft), the highest mountain in Crete. The modern name of Psiloritis (the High Mountain), which is given to the whole massif of Idha, fits it well, for from whatever side it is seen, it is instantly recognisable and clearly dominant. The trees from which it derived its ancient name of Idha (old Doric for a timber tree) have gone, and the slopes below the tree-line are bare or at most scrub-covered.

On the flanks of the mountain are many villages, up to the limit where year-round cultivation is possible. The most famous of these, on the north side at 740 metres (2,428ft), is Anóyia (Upland) whose inhabitants rivalled the Sphakiots as defenders of faith and freedom. Around the village can be seen many agricultural terraces with dams for soil and moisture conservation, of great antiquity and no longer in use. Some of these terraces may be associated with the Minoan settlement on this site.

Above Anoyia, and now accessible by a motorable track, is the Plain of Nídha. This is surrounded by the highest peaks of the Idha massif, and is the highest of the large elevated plateaux of Crete. Its floor, at 1,667 metres (5,469ft), is covered with scrub and large stones in the south-western part, but elsewhere level and consisting of reddish-yellow alluvial soil. For about half the year, Nidha is covered with snow, but each summer lush vegetation springs up to cover it, and the herdsmen of Anoyia prize it as a pasture. On the steep slope of Psiloritis,

TOPOGRAPHY AND GEOLOGY

above the north-western side of the plain, is the Idaean Cave—in ancient times a sanctuary of Zeus, in modern times a refuge for guerillas. The plain has no natural drainage except by means of swallow-holes; it is approached from Anoyia over a col, and the track at the south end which leads down to the Messara also passes over higher ground where it leaves the plain.

On the eastern slope of Psiloritis are the villages of Krousónas at 460 metres (1,509ft) and Ayia Varvára at 580 metres (1,903ft); farther round the mountain to the south, where it falls away towards the Messara, is the little mountain plain of Gérgeri at 520 metres (1,706ft), and west of it the village of Záros at 340 metres (1,115ft). Both are famous for their large perennial springs. Above the village of Zaros, to the north, is the monastery of Vrondísi, which perches on a shelf on the mountainside and has a spring of its own. Farther to the north-west, a string of villages lines the western flank of the mountain and many of these, too, have their own large springs. Most of these are contact springs at local contacts between the massive limestones of Psiloritis and underlying impervious rocks, usually metamorphic basement material. The whole mass of Psiloritis, so dry on its high limestone slopes, acts as a large subterranean reservoir, supplying the water to the springs of the surrounding villages.

CENTRAL CRETE

With the abrupt fall from the limestone heights of Psiloritis, western Crete is left behind. Eastward and southward is landscape of a different kind. As far as Lassíthi and Mt Dhíkti the hills and deep-cut valleys which border the coastal plain are more gentle in their form, shaped by water and wind to softer outlines. Olive trees and vines cover the land, the olives always dark against the golden soil, the green of the vines vivid and translucent at first, then darkening through the summer. The soils here are among the most deep and fertile in the island, derived from the underlying Tertiary marls and softer limestones. In some districts, however, these light-coloured marls

CRETE

and rendzinas give way to heavier clay soils, as in the plain of Kastélli Pedhiádhos.

In this central area, where the island is at its widest, the longitudinal mountain spine of Crete can be traced only in the low rounded hills south of Arkhánes and the Pedhiádha. To the north of these gentle hills, lie the low ridges and broad valleys which stretch in a parallel series trending north-south from Týlissos, below the foot of Psiloritis in the west, past Knossos to Episkopí, at the western ridge of Pedhiadha. Steep-sided Iuktas alone stands out: a solitary rocky mass dominating the vineyards. At the foot of Iuktas lies Arkhanes, separated by the broad, fertile plain of Pedhiadha from the high wall of the Lassithi Mountains and the shoulder of Dhikti, black with cloud.

The North Coast

From the high, steep cliffs of Rogdhia, at the foot of which is the great salt spring of Almyrós, to the city of Iraklion there is only a narrow coastal strip to which the new National Road is

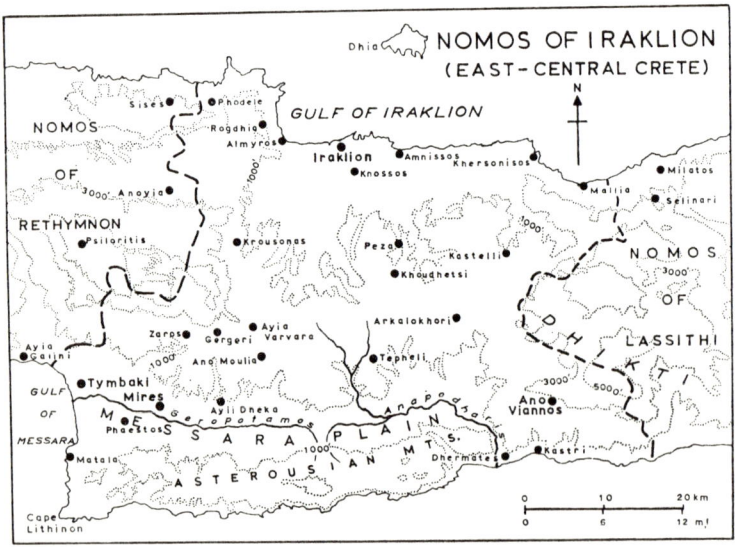

TOPOGRAPHY AND GEOLOGY

bringing tourists and development. The Gulf of Iraklion extends from Rogdhia to the high land of Póros which protects Iraklion harbour on the east side. The barren island of Dhía affords some shelter from the seas raised by a north or northeast wind, but the harbour lacks natural protection on its western side. East of Poros the coastal plain is wider, up to 5 kilometres in some places, and extends eastwards as far as the gorge of Selinári, where it meets the northern spurs of Dhikti. This plain is remarkable, even in Crete, for the intensity with which it has been developed from the earliest period. At its eastern end is Mállia, in Minoan times the rival of Knossos in art and opulence. There were ports at Khersónisos and Amnissós, where also was the priestly factory for Minoan amulets, prized no doubt by expectant mothers throughout the Aegean. Even Mílatos, the hill town to the east, was numbered by Homer with Knossos, Górtys and Phaistós. In modern times, intensive farming and improved communications, including the new international airport of Iraklion, have brought the prosperity of the plain to a new height.

South-Central Crete

This part of the island comprises four distinct topographical units. These are, from north to south, the descent from the central ridge down through a hill zone to the Messara Plain, the Messara Plain itself, the Asteroúsian Mountains which form its southern boundary, and the south coast of the island.

The main approach to the Messara Plain from Iraklion in the north is over a col above Ano Moúlia. Here the road cuts through thick marls resting insecurely in places upon impervious clays. Local landslides and slumping are common features of the area, particularly after periods of heavy rain. From the point at which the steep descent to Ayii Dhéka begins, almost the whole of the Messara can be seen. Lying to the west, in the direction of the Gulf, are Gortys, once the Roman capital of Crete, and Míres, a new commercial and administrative centre. Beyond Mires is the hill of Phaistos, with its Minoan palace and, almost on the shore of the Gulf, the tomato boom-town of Tymbáki with only the beach of Kókkinos Pírgos (Red Tower) beyond it. Eastwards from Ayii Dheka, the plain slopes slightly upwards to the watershed, and then falls away and narrows beyond Kharakás, at the head of the valley of the Anapodháris. Kharakas marks the southern terminal of another through route from Iraklion in the north. This road climbs up past Knossos and through the slopes and valleys of Kounávi and Khoudhétsi, to a high pass above Tephéli. A third route, farther to the east, branches off at Pezá, goes to Arkalokhóri and then skirts the steep limestone flank of Dhikti to Ano Viánnos, before running down to the sea at Kastrí on the southern coast.

The Plain of Messara, as a topographical unit, is the largest lowland area in Crete, with a west-east length of 50 kilometres and a north-south width of up to 10 kilometres. Thirty kilometres eastward from the Gulf of Messara the plain is divided into a western and an eastern half by the low watershed of the River Geropótamos, flowing westward into the Gulf, and the Anapodharis (Upside-down River) which flows to the east. This river falls into the Libyan Sea through a cleft in the east end of the Asterousian Mountains near Dhermátes. Of the two rivers, the Geropotamos (Strong River) alone is perennial, and then only in its lower course, where it is fed by the springs of Zaros and Gergeri. In the western part of the Geropotamos valley many thousands of shallow wells provide water to irrigate the plain. These become less frequent as the land rises, and much less irrigation is practised in the eastern parts of the plain. Comprehensive irrigation schemes tapping deeper aquifers are now being carried out throughout the plain.

The plain supports a large number of villages, many of which lie at its southern margin, against the north-facing slopes of the Asterousian Mountains. These mountains run along the southern coast of central Crete from Cape Lithinón (the Stony) in the west until they merge into the mass of Dhikti 50 kilometres to the east. Throughout their length they exhibit towards

1 Dry farming of cereals and olives near Gournia

2 *(above)* Khania: an aerial view of the town, taken in May 1945 immediately after the end of World War II. The heavily bombed areas stand out as large white patches. The Venetian harbours and the line of the Venetian walls and ditch can clearly be seen, together with the cruciform plan of the Municipal Market and the grid-iron street patterns of the modern suburbs; *(below)* hills bordering the Messara Plain and rising northward to the distant peaks of Mt Idha (Psiloriti)

TOPOGRAPHY AND GEOLOGY

the Libyan Sea an almost unbroken line of cliffs. St Paul was neither the first nor the last to be shipwrecked off these shores.

At Cape Lithinon the coast turns northwards towards Ayia Galini, forming the Gulf of Messara. Here the character of the coastline changes, with a large curving bay forming a major break between long stretches of cliff to west and east. The bay itself is completely exposed and has never offered other than a fair-weather anchorage. The main Roman port for the plain lay to the south of the Gulf in the small cove of Mátala, with its fine pebbly beach and dramatic line of cave-studded cliffs.

The Lassithi Mountains (Dhikti)

To the east of the Messara Plain, Dhikti—2,148 metres (7,048ft)—and the mountains of Lassithi form a solid barrier across the island from the Libyan Sea to the cliffs of Milatos in the north. The traveller has a choice of only two routes from Iraklion to the eastern Eparchies of Crete. One is the short northern route through the once-dangerous gorge of Selinari; the other is over the peaks of the Lassithi mountains, across Lassithi plain, and down the northern face of Dhikti. Both routes lead to Neápolis and Ayios Nikolaos. The Lassithi route climbs slowly to Avdhóu, and from there more steeply, following the side of a steep gorge up to a col set with rows of old stone windmills. To the north one sees the outline of the Gulf of Mallia, over 1,000 metres (3,281ft) below; to the south, there is a short gentle descent to the floor of the plateau of Lassithi 950 metres (3,117ft) above sea level.

This plateau is one of the most striking physical features of Crete. It has a flat alluvial surface measuring 15 kilometres from east to west, and 10 kilometres from north to south. At the eastern end the regularity of the plain is broken by several conical limestone hills standing up from its surface, whilst the whole is surrounded in an unbroken circle by the high grey peaks of Dhikti. Drainage is by one main series of *katavothras* at the eastern end of the plain. These are often unable to cope with

CRETE

the spring meltwater and parts of the plain, especially in the west where the surface is lower, are flooded each year. In summer, however, the water table is low enough for irrigation to be needed. A rectangular pattern of drainage and irrigation ditches in the western part of the plain is attributed by some to the Romans; today, every field has its windpump, and the plain is famous for the thousands of windmills which display their white sails in the summer sunlight. Each year the number of windpumps still in use diminishes as they are gradually replaced by electric and engine-driven pumps.

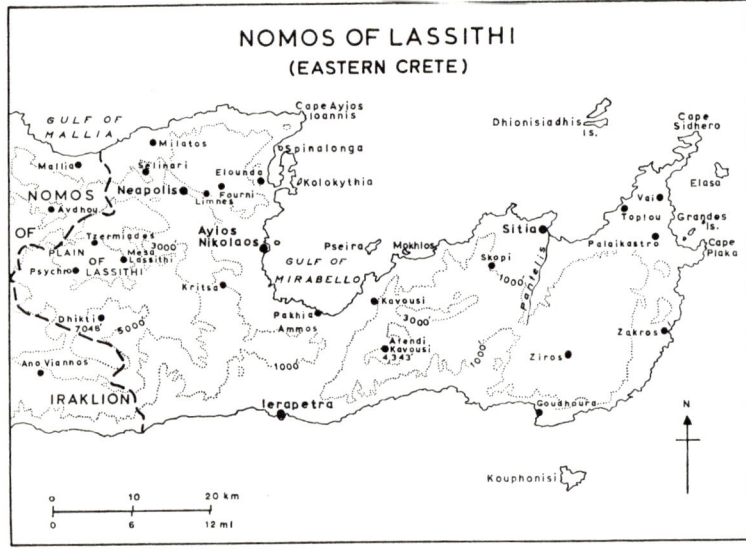

The plain is inhabited throughout the year, although winters are severe; villages being spread round the plateau edge above the level of the annual floods. High up above the village of Psychró on the south side of the plateau, where Dhikti rises steeply, is the cave in which tradition holds that Zeus was born. The road crossing the plain passes through Tzermiádes, the largest village, and runs eastwards to the pass above the monastery of Kroustallínia and the developing village of Mésa

TOPOGRAPHY AND GEOLOGY

Lassithi. From the col a last view of the plain and its surrounding mountains precedes the descent to the plains of Neapolis and Límnes in the north-east.

The alternative route to Neapolis and Ayios Nikolaos does not cross the central mountain block, but runs through the gorge of Selinari. This narrow defile is approached from the coastal plain beyond Mallia and, until 1971, the road which passed through it was notorious for its daemonic hazards. The road ran on a narrow ledge along the south side of the chasm leading up to the monastery of St George of Selinari, where every traveller stopped to give thanks for a safe passage and to ask for the saint's protection on the road ahead. Now the monastery is by-passed and the new National Road takes a lower course and drives, with cuttings, embankments and one tunnel, straight for Neapolis. The bottom of the gorge is half-filled with debris and many of its features, including two old water-mills, have been destroyed. Although the saint's protection may be needed no longer, a place of beauty has been lost for ever.

East of Selinari there is a pass, under which the new road tunnels, and from which can be seen the broad plain of Neapolis. The town itself stands on a spur jutting in from the south, and is conspicuous for its handsome modern church, new school and sports stadium. To the east of the town, which is by-passed by the new road, the plain narrows and two rows of old stone windmills stand on spurs on the northern side. The road then traverses the small plain of Limnes, out of which a pass leads over to Ayios Nikolaos.

North of Limnes the ground rises steeply to the mountainous triangle of land lying between Milatos, Ayios Nikolaos and Cape Ayios Ioánnis (St John). Here the limestone ridges enclose steep-sided valleys, and near the middle of the triangle lies the village of Fourní, on the edge of a perfect little polje set in green yet rugged hills. Fourni is reached by a road branching off northwards from the main road just west of Limnes; from Fourni a pass, complete with attendant windmills, crosses the

CRETE

easternmost ridge, and the Bay of Spinalónga (Long Thorn) and the salterns of Elounda are seen spread out below. The Venetian fortress of Spinalonga on its tiny islet guards the entrance to the bay which is protected from the sea by a long low parallel offshore island also called Spinalonga (see Appendix B). At the head of the bay, beyond the salterns and the stone tourist-chalets of Elounda Beach, is a high headland which conceals Ayios Nikolaos and the Gulf of Mirabéllo.

EASTERN CRETE

The Isthmus of Ierápetra
At the eastern edge of Dhikti, the landscape of Crete undergoes a complete character change. The island narrows to a north-south width of less than 15 kilometres for about 13 kilometres, forming the Isthmus of Ierapetra. It is only here, in this low square of land separating Dhikti from the Sitia mountains to the east, that the central mountain spine of Crete is completely absent. Formed at least partially by faulting and composed of marine Upper Tertiary deposits, the isthmus is drained to north and south from a low central watershed at 125 metres (410ft).

The northern shore of the isthmus forms the head of the Gulf of Mirabello, on the western shores of which lies Ayios Nikolaos, the largest town of eastern Crete. It stands on high ground above its harbour and around a picturesque circular lake, backed by cliffs and connected to the main harbour by a narrow channel, through which run out the waters of a submerged spring. The port is protected to some extent by the offshore island of Ayios Nikolaos, with its flashing beacon and its chapel. At the head of the bay, in the south-west corner of the isthmus, lies Pakhía Ámmos (Thick Sand), a prosperous port-village in the days of the coasting trade, before Crete had roads for wheeled traffic. Both village and harbour suffered almost total destruction in World War II, from which neither has yet fully recovered.

TOPOGRAPHY AND GEOLOGY

From Pakhia Ammos, the mountains of Sitia can be seen to the south-east, rising in a monolithic cliff to almost 1,000 metres (3,281ft) along the eastern side of the isthmus. Its impact is made still more dramatic by the shadowy gorge which cuts the precipice almost to its base below the flat top of Kapsás, 1,002 metres (3,287ft). In sudden contrast, the isthmus lies low and green beneath, its gentle undulations dwarfed on either side. The natural corridor of the isthmus leads one through to the south coast and thus to the town and port of Ierapetra, lying on the western side of a small sandy bay and dominated by a high cliff to the east. This is surmounted by a monastery, and is the holy rock from which the town gets its name. Around Ierapetra the isthmus forms an area of fertile and well-watered land. In recent years this has been intensively cultivated, taking advantage of the hot climate and sheltered location, and it has now an international trade in early-season produce, particularly tomatoes.

The South and East Coasts

The coastal plain of Ierapetra is the only break of any significance in the steep and rugged coastline extending along the south coast of the island from Cape Lithinon, at the western end of the Asterousia range, to Cape Goudhoúra in the east. A short distance east of Goudhoura the coast turns northward and continues cliff-lined with few breaks to the north-eastern tip of Crete, Cape Sídhero (the Headland of Iron). About 20 kilometres north-east from Goudhoura is the site of the Minoan palace of Zákros, on a tiny coastal plain at the mouth of a narrow and impressive gorge. Twelve kilometres north of Zakros, Cape Pláka (the Flat Rock) forms the southern side of the Bay of Grándes, in which a group of islands lies off the Minoan settlement of Palaíkastro. The bay sweeps round to the north, past the palm beach of Vaï to Cape Sidhero 20 kilometres to the north.

CRETE

The Sitia District

East of Pakhia Ammos, Crete consists of high mountains enclosing steep-sided valleys, not all of which reach the sea. The main orientation of the valleys is north-south, and their slopes produce some of the best wine grapes in Crete. Above Mokhlos on the north coast can be seen the white gashes of anhydrite quarries. Sitia, the administrative centre of the Eparchy, is built on a steep slope on the western angle of the Bay of Sitia, with fine prospects eastwards towards Cape Sidhero and inland up the fertile valley of the Pantélis river. This river is dry in summer, but wells in the valley bottom provide abundant water for the irrigation of the valley and beyond, so that even in summer the land is green.

East of the valley of the Pantelis and of the Gulf of Sitia, where the island is about 27 kilometres wide, Crete is little but a barren and stony waste. There are few villages and most of the land is a karstic limestone plateau with a general level of 600–700 metres (1,969–2,297ft). Near the centre of the plateau is the small polje of Zíros, surrounded by a natural limestone wall. The yellow clay soils of the polje are well cultivated, and the greenness contrasts vividly with the barren greyness of the surrounding karst. The limestone plateau extends to within about a kilometre of the sea, to which it falls away steeply on both the north and south coasts. On the north-east there is a steep descent to the cliff-bound peninsula of Toplóu in the centre of which stands the monastery, 160 metres (525ft) above the sea and surrounded by its cultivated fields. Six kilometres to the north-east, across the broken and almost bare limestone hillocks of the peninsula, lies the little sandy bay of Vai, with a grove of date palms growing along its shores (see page 48). The chief characteristics of the high land east of Sitia are that it is dry, uninviting and hard of access, but like other such regions it has many beauties.

3 CLIMATE, VEGETATION AND LAND USE

IN spite of Crete's proximity to the northern shores of Africa and to the Near East, the island's climate is relatively mild, with marked local variations ranging from sub-tropical to sub-alpine. As the climate varies, so also does the natural vegetation and land cultivation, so that a number of visually distinctive zones are formed.

CLIMATIC CONDITIONS

The coastal plains
Table 1 shows the weather characteristics of the coastal area which attracts some 95 per cent of the tourists who visit Crete and gives them their impressions of the island as a sun-drenched paradise. It indicates the range of temperatures normally experienced during the year at Iraklion, the principal city and port.

Only four months, from December to March inclusive, have mean monthly temperatures below 15° C (59° F). This is the period of the Cretan winter—a bad time in spite of its mildness —and coinciding with the rainy season which lasts from November to March, with a pronounced maximum of precipitation in December and January. Much of the rainfall is torrential, occurring as sharp, heavy thunderstorms of relatively short duration. In between the stormy spells and the few grey days, there are warm, clear periods, free from haze, bright and sunny,

CRETE

Table 1

TEMPERATURE AND RAINFALL: IRAKLION

Month	Average temperature °C (°F)		Average rainfall mm (in)		Rainy days
January	12	(54)	94	(3·7)	14
February	12	(54)	76	(3·0)	12
March	14	(57)	41	(1·6)	7
April	17	(62)	23	(0·9)	4
May	20	(68)	18	(0·7)	3
June	23	(74)	3	(0·1)	0·7
July	26	(78)	0	(0·0)	0·1
August	26	(78)	3	(0·1)	0·4
September	24	(75)	18	(0·7)	2
October	21	(69)	43	(1·7)	5
November	17	(63)	69	(2·7)	8
December	14	(58)	102	(4·0)	13
Year	*19*	*(66)*	*490*	*(19·2)*	*69·2*

when the eye is drawn from the gold of the ripening oranges in the coastal plains, and is caught and held by the dazzling brilliance of needle-sharp snow on mountains some 30–50 kilometres away, whose peaks cut into a sky alive with light and cloud. These are the memorable days, among the best which Crete has to offer.

In the summer, except sometimes at dawn, the long, clear views are lost. Heat hazes reduce visibility and confine the attention to closer landscapes. In distant views, although the outlines may remain, the detail cannot be clearly discerned.

During the eight long months of the Cretan summer, several variations in weather type occur, resulting chiefly from fluctuations in temperature. Monthly means rise from 17° C (62° F)

CLIMATE, VEGETATION AND LAND USE

in April to a maximum in July and August of 26° C (78° F) and then gradually decrease to 17° C (63° F) in November. The normal daily pattern is of fairly hot temperatures in the range of 16–32° C (60–90° F), with a peak shortly after midday, and of pleasantly warm early mornings (before 9 am) and late afternoons and evenings (after 5 pm). These air temperatures occur with a low relative humidity of 60–65 per cent, and there are long periods of clear skies and uninterrupted sunshine.

The absence of rain during the Cretan summer, although not without its problems for farmers, makes the area attractive to foreign visitors and local people alike. Each town and village has a particular street or square where for a couple of hours each evening, especially on Sundays, the population congregates to talk and stroll, to see and be seen. Tables outside the cafés and restaurants compete with the crowds for the available space. The cinemas, too, move out into the open air for their summer season.

Life on the coastal plains alternates between the outdoor routine of the summer months, with its long siestas and its longer evenings, and the more moderate but less appreciated regime of winter. This typically Mediterranean climate can be found in Crete not only in Iraklion but, with only minor modifications, throughout the coastal areas and in most parts of the island below 800 metres (2,625ft) above sea level.

The hill zone

The land lying above the coastal plains and below heights of 800 metres (2,625ft) covers about two-thirds of the surface area of the island.

Table 2 shows the differences in weather type as one moves away from coastal localities, such as Iraklion, up into the hills. Anoyia, at a height of 740 metres (2,428ft), is some 30 kilometres west-south-west of Iraklion, on the northern slopes of Psiloritis. Summer temperatures remain high in this zone, with monthly averages a few degrees lower than in Iraklion, but the winters become much cooler. Mean temperatures remain well above

43

CRETE

freezing, although the average figures mask a few days with sub-zero temperatures and quite severe frosts.

Perhaps the most striking contrast between the coasts and the hill zone is the marked increase in rainfall. The mean annual total at Anoyia—1,115mm (43·9in)—is more than double the average for Iraklion. A prolonged rainy season, lasting from

Table 2

TEMPERATURE AND RAINFALL: ANOYIA

Month	Average temperature °C (°F)		Average rainfall mm (in)		Rainy days	Frequency of thunderstorms days/1,000
January	7	(45)	211	(8·3)	22·2	58·1
February	7	(44)	170	(6·7)	17·9	50·9
March	9	(49)	119	(4·7)	15·1	32·3
April	13	(56)	53	(2·1)	10·1	37·8
May	16	(61)	61	(2·4)	8·6	38·7
June	21	(70)	5	(0·2)	2·6	15·6
July	23	(73)	3	(0·1)	0·5	2·2
August	22	(72)	15	(0·6)	1·6	2·2
September	19	(67)	18	(0·7)	4·4	31·1
October	16	(61)	71	(2·8)	10·3	88·2
November	13	(55)	158	(6·2)	15·1	66·7
December	9	(48)	231	(9·1)	21·2	73·1
Year	*14*	*(58)*	*1,115*	*(43·9)*	*129·7*	*41·4*

Percentage frequency days of frost

November	0·8
December	1·8
January	6·5
February	12·1
March	3·8
April	0·6

Period November–April: 4·3

CLIMATE, VEGETATION AND LAND USE

October until May, curtails the dry season which is here reduced to a mere four months.

The high mountain zone

Above the coastal plains and the terraced hillsides stand the high mountains—a land apart. Here the Mediterranean climate does not extend; conditions are either cool temperate or subalpine, rainfall is much higher and there is an exaggerated contrast between the winter and summer seasons.

During the winter months the mountains are covered with snow, the snowline being about 600 metres (2,000ft) above sea level. The high mountain plains of Omalos—1,140 metres (3,740ft)—and Nidha—1,667 metres (5,469ft)—neither of which is permanently inhabited, are often snowcovered until about April, whilst the lower inhabited plateau of Lassithi—950 metres (3,117ft) is usually clear by March. The snow generally lies on the high peaks until May, forming a crystal-white divide between the blue summer sky and the green, vine-covered hillsides. From June until October the mountains are mostly snow-free, although small patches may linger in crevices or in the shade of boulders.

PLANT LIFE AND CULTIVATION

The coastal zone

The coastal plains of Crete, with their warm almost subtropical climate and their fertile alluvial soils, are the richest parts of the island. For millennia now, the land has been cleared, the fields delineated and the crops sown and harvested. Today cultivation is at its most intensive in these areas; the long growing season permits double cropping, and the use of local groundwater for irrigation guarantees high yields. Field sizes tend to be small and land values extremely high, particularly along the coast itself where farmers compete for the land, usually unsuccessfully, with the builders of new hotels and other tourist facilities.

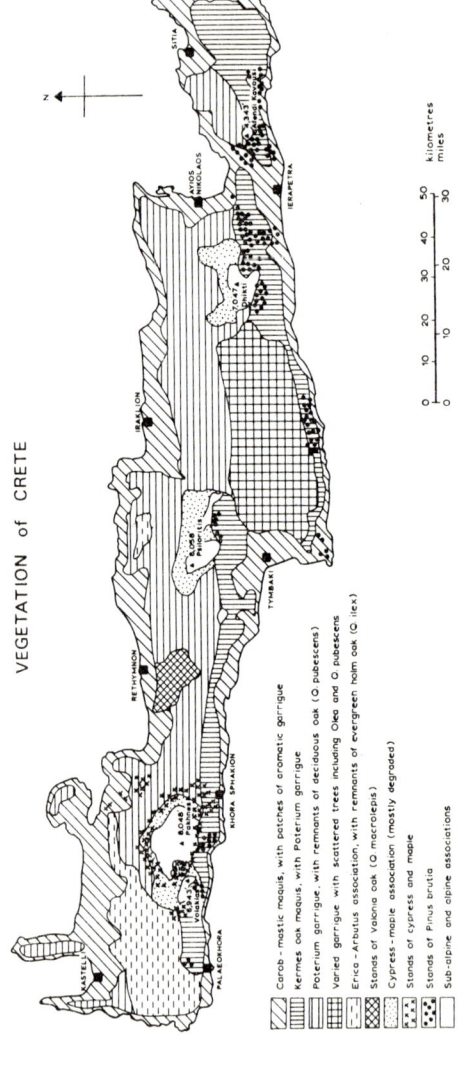

CLIMATE, VEGETATION AND LAND USE

In the agricultural areas, the landscape is a varied mosaic of cultivated crops, alternating on poorer ground with maquis and patches of dwarf shrub associations. The two most characteristic plants of the Cretan maquis are the mastic bush (*Pistacia lentiscus*) and the carob tree (*Ceratonia siliqua*). The carob is an easily recognisable, robust, sturdy tree with a thick trunk, spreading branches and dark green leathery foliage. Long broad pods, known as locust beans, grow straight out from the branches and upper parts of the trunk in the spring and summer months; they are green at first, but dry to a dark brown colour. These pods have a high sugar content and are sometimes fed to animals. The trees are well adapted to survival through long periods of drought in poor rocky conditions and even in the most unpromising situations large specimens flourish, often reaching 10 metres (33ft) in height.

By comparison, the mastic bush is relatively small, rarely exceeding 3 metres (10ft) in height. Like the carob, it is an evergreen with dark spreading leaves. It can be recognised by its strongly acrid, resinous smell, and by its cluster of red berries which are gradually blackened by the heat of the summer.

Various other shrubs, flowers and small trees occur in the maquis, their importance varying in different parts of the island. One plant which is common near the coasts is the agave or century plant, *Agave americana*. Native to Mexico but naturalised in the Mediterranean for over two centuries, it has enormous cactus-like rosettes of huge thick bluish-green leaves up to 2 metres (7ft) long, with sharp spines along their edges. Once in the plant's lifetime, after ten to fifteen years' growth, a tall stem grows from the centre of the rosette, ending in a candelabra-like flower-head consisting of hundreds of green and yellow florets. The flower-stem grows at a fantastic rate, reaching a height of 10 metres (33ft) in a month. After flowering, the plant dies.

Where the maquis has been destroyed by clearance or overgrazing, smaller shrub communities have often been able to recolonise all or part of the site and to establish themselves successfully. The characteristic shrub community of the lowlands is a form of garrigue dominated by aromatic plants, such as the thyme-like *Coridothymus capitatus*, and flowering shrubs, such as the rock rose (*Cistus villosus*). Many of these shrubs survive in spite of heavy grazing because they are well-armoured with long hard spines; others, like the asphodel, are unpalatable to animals.

The garrigue occurs most frequently in the more remote and infertile areas, in a man-and animal-modified form, but in the coastal plains themselves it has been almost entirely replaced by food crops. In some sheltered areas, conditions are virtually sub-tropical: a grove of palm trees, thought to have been introduced by the Arabs in the ninth century, flourishes and reproduces on the sandy beach of Vai in eastern Crete. Farther west, on the north coast at Mallia, extensive banana plantations, protected by windbreaks, add another touch of tropical lushness to the landscape.

The tradition of specialisation is well established, each of the coastal plains being associated with the production of one or more particular crops. As Mallia is linked with bananas, so is Khania with orange production, Rethymnon with its peanuts, and the coastal plains of Ierapetra and the Messara with tomatoes. The cultivation of early and late vegetables, particularly the summer staples of tomatoes and cucumbers, is an outstanding growth point in many areas, including the coastal plain near Khersonisos, close to the urban market of Iraklion. Polythene greenhouses, which catch the eye as the summer sun is reflected from their shiny surfaces, are a conspicuous feature of this kind of farming.

All the usual Mediterranean crops, such as vines, olives and cereals, are grown in the coastal area, together with certain cool-temperate crops, such as potatoes and other vegetables. Where vines are grown in fertile lowland areas, specialisation is usual in either table grapes or sultanas, both principally for export.

CLIMATE, VEGETATION AND LAND USE

The hill zone
Virtually all the former forests of Crete have been destroyed: cleared by local people for fuel and in the making of fields, and felled for export at least from Hellenic times onwards. The scrub which grew up in the cleared areas has been prevented from regenerating into woodland both by continued cutting for fuel and by the devastating attentions of almost $\frac{3}{4}$ million sheep and goats (741,377 in 1966). Unfortunately, of all the regions of Greece, Crete has been by far the most backward in pursuing a serious programme of re-afforestation.

In the hill zone, therefore, the main associations are again carob-mastic maquis and the very mixed garrigue, less than a metre in height, which is characterised by a variety of flowering shrubs, scented herbs and spiny plants. That compact hemispherical cushion of spikes, *Poterium spinosum*, is the sole dominant in large areas of the upper hill garrigue. With other spiny associates, such as the thorny broom (*Calycotome villosa*), it shows a hostile front to the would-be hill-walker. It is shunned by the sheep and goats which of necessity are capable of eating most things and, as the tastier vegetation is gradually grazed out of existence, the area of *Poterium* gradually expands. Although a curiosity to the traveller, this plant represents a serious and increasing threat to the Cretan pastures, the quality of which deteriorates each season.

Broad expanses of maquis are found in the upper hill zone throughout the island, dominated by one or other of the evergreen Mediterranean oaks. The kermes oak (*Quercus coccifera*) is the most widespread variety, occurring throughout the length of the island on the southern slopes of the main mountain ranges. When protected from grazing it will grow into a small tree, with small leathery holly-like leaves, bright green and shiny, and ovoid acorns in prickly cups.

The other main kind of hill maquis is dominated by the evergreen holm oak (*Q. ilex*) which sometimes grows to the size of a small tree; it is very similar to the kermes oak except that its leaves are mostly non-spiny and have white or grey hairy lower surfaces.

Scattered among the maquis are many different fruit trees. The olive is by far the most important; with a total of 17 million trees, it is by a large margin the most common tree on the island. Also characteristic of the hill zone is the almond, its sweetly scented pink and white flowers a major attraction in early spring. In a few areas, such as the plain of Neapolis in eastern Crete, the light green leaves of the almond are more in evidence than the grey-green of the olive. Here, as elsewhere in Greece and in the Near East, almonds are used to make a syrup of the milk of almonds, perfumed with orange-blossom water. This syrup is diluted with hot or cold water to form a very fine, sweet, delicately scented, non-alcoholic drink known as *soumádha*.

Most of the farmers in Crete make their living among the almonds and the olives in the ridges and valleys of this broad hill zone; both trees demand and receive very little attention during the year other than at times of harvest. A much greater share of the farmer's time is given to his vines which are tended with all the love and care and attention to detail of a good gardener. Early each spring the vines are pruned and the ground between them is carefully turned over; by March the vivid yellow-green of the young vine leaves, translucent in the spring sunshine, announces the end of winter and the beginning of a new season. The young shoots grow rapidly, and the first tiny fruits set some three months later. Then follows a long slow process of growth and maturing which culminates in a harvest season ranging from mid-July, for some of the early table-grapes near Iraklion, through to October for much of the wine vintage on the higher slopes.

The summer is a busy time for the farmer who will be out checking his vines for signs of mildew, or perhaps giving them the benefit of one last irrigation. During the vintage or harvest itself, whole families work long days in the fields, gathering the grapes. The sultanas are laid out to dry in the sun on special

3 *(above)* Ayia Triadha: the site of the Minoan palace, overlooking the western part of the Messara Plain; *(below)* Phaistos: part of the Minoan site

4 Churches: *(above)* the ruined fourth-century church of St Titus in the remains of the Roman city of Gortys; *(below)* the church at Panormos

CLIMATE, VEGETATION AND LAND USE

racks and on covers spread out in the corners of fields; the table grapes and wine grapes are transported immediately to the markets, the packing centres and the wine presses. Following the harvest, the leaves wither on the stocks, and the vineyards wear an abandoned look until the time-honoured cycle begins anew the following year.

The rich vineyards on the fertile slopes give way on poorer ground to small patches of wheat, barley or other cereals. Winter fodder crops such as vetches are also seen. Both these and the cereals are sown in late autumn and have completed their growth by the time the winter rains end. Harvest time is as early as May near the sea and as late as June or early July up in the mountains where the summer is later.

The cereals, the vines, the olives and other fruit trees form a close mesh of cultivation over the hillsides. Slopes of surprising steepness are planted with rows of olives and vines, often with a casual disregard for the problems of soil erosion. It is quite common for slopes of up to 1-in-3 to be cultivated, although in most cases the steeper slopes are terraced. A little modern terracing has been done with bulldozers, and the resultant regular contouring is a feature of certain hillsides, as near Arkalokhori and in the Sitia district. The great majority of the terraces, however, belong to former centuries and are today uncultivated. Constructed by hand, they are characterised by their intricate irregularity of form and their relative inaccessibility. A few of these old terraces are still in use, following the traditions of millennia rather than merely of centuries. They are reached on foot, cultivated using simple hand-tools, and their produce is carried down in the summer evenings on donkey or mule-back to the villages.

The high mountain zone

Characteristic of this cold, mountain zone are the occasional scattered stands of forest trees which survive in more or less degraded form, in various isolated localities. Between 800 and 1,200 metres (2,625–3,937ft) the pine (*Pinus brutia*) is most

CRETE

common, the largest stands being found in south-east Crete, on the light-coloured rendzinas.

Between 1,000 and 1,500 metres (3,281–4,921ft) and occasionally down to 800 metres (2,625ft), the principal vegetation is a cypress-maple combination (*Cupressus sempervirens*, var. *horizontalis* and *Acer orientalis*). The largest surviving stands of cypress are to be found in a belt ringing the Lefka Ori, some individual trees reaching 20 metres (66ft) in height. In most places, however, the maple has been badly degraded by grazing.

In the upper zones a mixture of late-spring and summer-flowering plants forms an intermittent low cover between the trees. These include the anemone (*Anemone hortensis*), with flowers ranging from scarlet and purple through the gentler shades to white; cyclamen (*Cyclamen hederifolium*); daphne (*Daphne oeloides*), and a spiny, violet-blue, thistle-like plant (*Eryngium creticum*).

Above the tree-line, at about 1,500 metres (4,921ft) above sea level, the sub-alpine zone proper begins. Here the vegetation consists of small, low-lying plants with a short summer growing season. These include a rock-cress and a number of bulbous plants, such as the Cretan tulip (*Tulipa cretica*), the yellow-eyed crocus (*Crocus sieberi*), and the appropriately named glory-of-the-snow (*Chionodoxa nana* and *C. cretica*).

Cultivation in the sub-alpine zone is non-existent, the sole use of the land being for rough summer grazing. Between 800 and 1,500 metres (2,625–4,921ft) the important cultivated areas are the mountain plains. Snow-covered in winter, in summer their brilliant green flat expanses, a mosaic of tiny fields, form an unforgettable contrast when seen against the dry, barren mountains which enclose and shelter them. On the mountainsides, the concept of 'fields' becomes meaningless in a regular and permanent sense. Tiny erratically shaped patches of ground, chosen for their soil cover, are sown to cereals or occupied by solitary fruit trees, such as the apple, plum or pear. In between these the bare rock surface, boulder-strewn and barren, forms the only field boundary and the only access road.

CLIMATE, VEGETATION AND LAND USE

Beyond these, the limits of cultivation, the sheep and goats range the mountain slopes in a never-ending food quest. After the winter snows have melted, the flocks move up into the mountains from their lowland pastures. They attack the brief-lived lush pastures, and then live a more frugal existence through the remainder of the summer until the first winter rains and snow drive them down from the high mountain peaks.

Polythene greenhouses

4   COMMUNICATIONS AND TRANSPORT

THE modern traveller in Crete nearly always journeys by road; the island has no railway and no domestic air service. Good modern roads link all the principal towns and villages, and there are excellent bus, taxi and car-hire services available. In the past, however, the longer and more difficult overland journeys were often avoided, sea travel being preferred wherever possible. Thus a considerable traffic developed in the transport of both goods and passengers by sea between the various ports of the island. This practice continued on a large scale until the 1940s, but declined rapidly following the development of a modern road network after World War II. Today there exists only one regular coastal shipping service, that between Ayios Nikolaos and Sitia, and even this is not a purely local service since it also links Crete to the Piraeus, Thira and Rhodes.

COASTAL SHIPPING

When coastal traffic was at its peak in the inter-war years, there were many vessels involved, varying in shape and size from caïques to small steamers. They plied between the principal north coast ports, linked the north and south coasts and, in the course of their circumnavigations, also called in at a large number of village-ports. Many of these were no more than conveniently situated bays with a storeroom built close by the shore, although some, like the now declining Pakhia Ammos near

COMMUNICATIONS AND TRANSPORT

Ayios Nikolaos, built quays and flourished for a period as small ports.

At most places, even on the more developed north coast, the steamers could not come alongside, but anchored offshore and transferred both passengers and freight to small boats. Such manoeuvres were rarely without incident, as shown by these extracts from a light-hearted account by Trevor-Battye of one particular coastal voyage in 1913:

> ... Such a boat runs weekly round the island of Crete, and on Tuesday, the 1st of June [1913], was lying outside the harbour of Canea, rolling badly in a considerable sea, when I reached her side after an unpleasant wetting, and took my passage for the coasting trip.
>
> The *S. Nikolas* is a steamer of 600 tons (net register), but, if I rightly understood her captain, able to carry 800 tons of cargo ... Right aft are the only passenger cabins, four in number, for the passengers in general sleep on deck, and a very motley crowd I found them. Cretans, Greeks, Italians, Egyptians, Turks, and Hebrews filled every corner. Each man had his bundle of food, and many had brought their bedding ...
>
> No boat in the coasting trade ever yet kept its time, and though the *S. Nikolas* was due to leave Canea at 10pm, there was so much loading and unloading of great casks of wine and olive-oil, of sulphur bags and barrels, of articles of household furniture and all the miscellany of a coaster's cargo, that we did not get off until long after midnight.
>
> The storm had suddenly died and there was a splendid moon, so that one could see the form of Akrotiri on the one hand and of Rhodopus on the other, as we slowly steamed towards Kolymbari, the village of the swimmers. Two little lights shone out over the water, but the village was asleep, and it was only after long delay and much blowing of the hooter, and shouting from the deck, that a boat was induced to come off for the few barrels and baskets we had brought for this place; but we lay rocking there for some time longer, and I went and lay down for sleep ...
>
> Standing south again we presently rounded cape St John (H. Ioannis), the south-western point of Crete, and were immediately in one of those squalls which are so frequent on the southern coast. The next place reached is Selino, the principal town of the

province that bears that name . . . The *S. Nikolas* drops a passenger or two at each point of call; and here and there picks one up. Sometimes there is but little to leave or take, sometimes nothing. Here, at Selino, we land a few passengers and take on board some sacks of flour . . .

Euroclydon—St Paul's wind—maintains its character to this day. This wicked mountain-wind from the north had been gradually increasing in strength, and now raised a sea that was quite nasty for small boats, and the poor fellows engaged in unloading [at Glakia] had a very unenviable time . . . These huge casks had to be brought up by the derrick from our hold and lowered over the ship's side into the sea, when they were taken charge of by the boatmen, and were then cleverly lashed together until quite a large raft had been formed of floating kegs, which was then towed ashore . . . But the most awkward things to handle were some big blocks of stone, for mill-stones, from the island of Melos, celebrated for its mill-stones from very ancient times. These had to be lowered into boats which were tossing about to such an extent that there was only just one particular fractional moment in their lively movements during which a stone could be checked and lowered into place. It was too rough for the men to stand upon the thwarts, and it really seemed as if bare feet must be smashed, if not a body flattened out.

Euroclydon increased; squall after squall fell from the mountains like a hammer on the sea. At 6.45 the big moon rose stately from the water, half an hour later night fell, and I saw little more of the coast till early on the following morning when we were entering the bay of Hierapetras . . . From Hierapetra the *S. Nikolas* returned by the way she had come, and I remained with her until we reached Sphakia.

ROADS

The ancient roads of Crete can still be traced throughout much of the island. Pioneer work on the identification of Minoan and classical routes was carried out in the 1930s by J. D. S. Pendlebury who traced established roads, protected by guard stations, linking most of the major settlement sites of these periods. In eastern Crete, for example, three main west-east routes linked the ancient cities of Palaikastro, Kato Zakros and Ampelos with the lowland isthmus of Ierapetra and places farther west. From

COMMUNICATIONS AND TRANSPORT

Knossos to Phaistos ran the main north-south road of central Crete, via Kanli Kastelli and Mires; it took Pendlebury, a fast walker, twelve hours to do this journey. Down in parts of the Messara Plain, between Mires and Praitória, the modern motor road closely follows the route of an earlier Roman road and long stretches of the Roman pavé could be seen while the new road was under construction. West of Knossos, the ancient road network is equally well developed and in all parts of Crete archaeologists as well as road-builders are now uncovering new evidence to add to Pendlebury's basic work.

During the Venetian occupation many of the roads carrying particularly heavy traffic, such as the main trunk routes and roads in the vicinity of the larger towns, were paved with stone to a width adequate for private carriages and goods carts. This provided an all-weather surface and did much to ensure the rapid movement of troops, equipment, supplies and produce between different parts of the island.

In the neighbourhood of Elounda through to the plain of Fourni, there are networks of roads, some paved and all suitable for pack animals. These roads are protected by a substantial stone wall on each side, and are particularly common in this part of Crete. It is possible, though uncertain, that they were built by the Venetians during the period when they held the island fortress of Spinalonga against the Turks, and that their purpose was to protect the mule-trains supplying foodstuffs from the small enclave on Crete then remaining to them.

The numerous complaints concerning the state of roads in Crete during the period of Turkish occupation suggest that their condition had seriously deteriorated by the late nineteenth century. Captain Spratt noted that in the mid-nineteenth century there were two possible routes from the west to Sitia, one along the north coast and one along the south coast from Ierapetra. The south coast route was considered locally to be the better of the two but even that is described by Spratt as a 'difficult and rocky mule-path', consistently 'bad and tiresome'.

CRETE

During the dry season, the roads were usually passable, but with the rocky nature of much of the terrain, the slowness and the heat, the longer journeys must have been tedious and uncomfortable. During autumn and winter, however, a sudden violent rainstorm could make travel impossible for periods lasting several days. In late October 1845, after a prolonged downpour, Victor Raulin had to wait for three days before the road from Ayia Rouméli to Omalos became passable: during the storms the road had become a torrent bed and the deep, swiftly moving water prevented all travel. According to Raulin, 'the roads were only really passable for mules and donkeys, and even the country people dismounted and led their animals down the steep slopes; the horses could not usually manage more than six and a half kilometres an hour; even on the highway from Khania to Megalo-Kastro (Iraklion) they could do no more than eight kilometres an hour'.

Other travellers, although more cheerful than Raulin, experienced similar difficulties. Trevor-Battye notes casually that at one point 'the horses had a hard time of it getting to Alíkambo, for the road had in places been washed away. One moment we were sliding down a slanting rock face with no foothold, and the next I had tumbled into a fountain, to the uncontrollable delight of the women who were dipping their water jars there.'

Early methods of travel

Until about fifty years ago, journeys between any two points on Crete were assessed in terms of time rather than distance; one thought of a journey of so many hours or days, calculated according to the speed of a man on foot and making allowances for the variation in terrain. Pendlebury, himself a great walker, says that 'Only those who have actually walked in the mountains can tell how misleading a map may be ... Distances are useless. Times alone matter.' Travelling on horse-back in 1913, Trevor-Battye noted that even a walker's time could be misleading for 'in travelling with pack-horses a five hour journey easily lengthens into one of seven'. Where pack-horses, mules and donkeys were heavily laden and travelling in long trains across difficult country, speeds were still further reduced.

The wealthier Cretans owned mules or horses, but most families possessed at least a donkey and as late as 1948 one half of all Cretan farmers marketed their products by mule or donkey pack. 'One constantly sees trains of these donkeys,' wrote Trevor-Battye, 'a skin full of oil hanging on either side of one, wine on another, charcoal and oranges on a third, pottery on a fourth, while living lambs, kids or poultry are carried in the same way. Sometimes the load quite conceals the donkey: one is a walking cornstack, while another is only betrayed by its bray beneath a towering load of scrub for fuel.'

The slowness of travel, the difficulties of communication, particularly in the mountain areas, and the problems of conveying perishable, heavy or bulky goods, such as most agricultural produce, did much to retard the economic development of Crete. Allbaugh cites the case of the village of Stavrochóri (Nomos of Lassithi) where spring waters that could have been used for the irrigation of profitable cash crops, such as bananas or early tomatoes, were allowed to run to waste. Although the crops could be grown, the village had no road in 1948, and produce could only be marketed after a bruising three-and-a-half-hour trek by donkey-pack, or by a one-hour donkey-pack and then a one-hour sea trip by caïque, which weather conditions often prevented.

The beginnings of modern transport

One of the earliest roads of the modern style was built in 1913 to connect an iron mine near Kolymbári with the port of Khania. At that time, the river Tavronítis west of Khania had just been spanned by a new girder bridge. The mine proved unprofitable, but the route remains in use.

The main motor roads linking the towns on the north coast were started during and after World War I. By 1922 the best road on the island, the tarmacadam road from Iraklion to Khania, was half completed. By 1935 there was a through road

CRETE

—of poor quality but nevertheless passable throughout the year —from Kastelli Kissamou in the west via Khania, Soudha, and Rethymnon to Iraklion. The 145-kilometre stretch from Khania to Iraklion took approximately three hours by car. In 1947 general neglect and wartime damage had caused such deterioration of the road surface that the trip took five hours' steady driving in a new American car, and buses were scheduled to take seven hours. The north coast road continued eastwards from Iraklion via Mallia and Selinari as far as Pakhia Ammos, whence an occasional truck would press on over a field track to Kavoúsi and sometimes beyond.

From Iraklion there was by the 1930s a road to Knossos on which one motor car ran a regular shuttle service or could be chartered for a special trip. It was an open five-seater Fiat and on its regular runs, from which it derived its name of *taktikí*, it seldom carried fewer than twelve adults and a small boy or two.

By 1948 the total length of the surfaced road network in Crete amounted to 1,384 kilometres (860 miles), most of it very rough. The pattern of roads (as shown on the map below) indicates a relatively high density network on the coastal plains of the north, but relatively few branch roads penetrating southwards through the mountains and almost no roads along the south coast. At that time, half the villages of Crete were

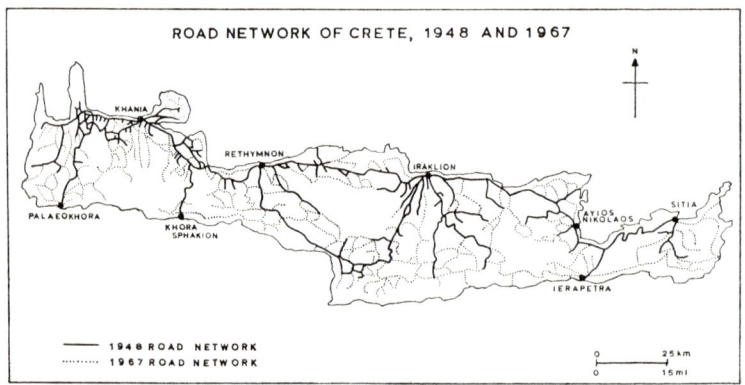

COMMUNICATIONS AND TRANSPORT

accessible only by mule-trail, and local public officials regarded roads as their second most important problem, after war.

Crete suffered heavily from bombing and other damage during World War II and the condition of the roads in the late 1940s was very bad indeed. By 1947 post-war recovery was only at a very early stage and the FAO Mission to Greece reported that speeds were necessarily reduced to an average of not more than 15 kilometres per hour. This is only about twice as fast as Raulin's estimate of the average speed of journeying in Crete on horse-back a century earlier. Speeds were kept down not only by the poor state of the roads but by the necessity of avoiding pedestrians, donkeys, mules, sheep and goats. In 1948 a mere 953 motor vehicles, including only sixty-four privately owned cars, battled noisily for right of way, against overwhelming odds, with some 60,000 mules and donkeys and countless pedestrians.

There were at that time 120 island taxis and 155 buses. Only about one-third of the villages had any kind of bus service, and there was a shortage of buses in all parts of the island, especially in the eastern and central districts. The inefficient practice of using trucks for passenger transport consequently became widespread. Of the 614 trucks on the island, 511 were available for hire, carrying both passengers and agricultural produce, and 103 were in private use.

The modern road networks

Apart from limited pioneer work during the inter-war period, the modern road system of Crete has been constructed almost entirely since 1948. The map on page 62 shows the extent of the present network of some 5,500 kilometres (3,418 miles) as it developed from the much smaller system of 1948. The principal axis of communication is still the northern coast road from Kastelli Kissamou to Ayios Nikolaos, now extending eastwards to Sitia. This is a national road having for most of its length at least the standard minimum width of 6 metres (20ft), with a tarmac surface and a well-engineered route. As recently as the early 1970s the original unwidened route of the 1920s was still in use in some sections, as between Stavroménos and Marathós. However, under the Cretan Development Plan of 1965, provision was made for a new Northern Axis Road. Construction began in the eastern half of the island with stretches of dual carriageway near Mallia and Pakhia Ammos and the construction of a new, superbly engineered section from Kavousi over the mountains to Sitia. A new route has been blasted through the Selinari gorge and across the Neapolis plain to Ayios Nikolaos, and by-passes have been provided for Iraklion and Rethymnon.

By the mid-1970s the Northern Axis was virtually complete and work was in progress on a new Southern Axis designed to provide, for the first time in the island's history, a good road along the length of the southern coast. At various points good link roads connect the two axes and give easy access to the interior of the island. It was also laid down as a guiding principle in planning that every village should have all-weather road access, together with all places of major archaeological, historical, scenic or other tourist interest. This programme is now virtually complete, although it cannot be claimed that all the minor roads are of uniform excellence. The provincial highways connecting the principal towns are all of a high standard as regards surface, width and general engineering, so also are the local roads to the larger villages and less remote archaeological sites. However, anyone planning to drive to the Idaean cave of Zeus, high on Psiloritis, must be prepared for a slow and somewhat bumpy ride.

The effect on Cretan village life of sudden and virtually total road access has been immense, both socially and commercially. Truck and bus services now reach nearly every settlement, so that perishable agricultural produce can be taken quickly to the urban markets, the processing and packing plants, and the refrigerated stores. Farmers and their families have much easier and more frequent access to the main towns for general family shopping, the purchase of specialised equipment, and the obtaining of expert advice, be it from the doctor, the lawyer or the agricultural extension worker.

Modern road transport

The 1948 figure of 953 motor vehicles had increased to 16,145 by 1969, as compared with 3,554 in 1963. The greatest increase has been in the number of trucks, of which there were 6,291 in 1969. These are supplemented by a growing number of mainland and foreign trucks, many of them refrigerated, which cross over to the island from Piraeus en route from Europe, Thessaloniki and Athens. In the private transport sector, there were 4,156 cars in 1969, as compared with 829 in 1963 and a mere 64 in 1948. The number increases year by year. Another popular form of transport is the motor cycle, usually of German or Japanese manufacture.

The *fréza* or single-axle tractor—of which there must be 15–20,000 in use in Crete—is a versatile machine. It has a two-stroke petrol engine mounted below handle-bars on a single axle to which is attached a rotovator blade for ploughing. The rotovator can, however, be detached and a pair of road wheels substituted; a two-wheel trailer, complete with seating, is then attached at the rear and the tractor becomes a road vehicle. These *frézas* can be used for carrying agricultural produce, for shopping or for a family outing; they are relatively inexpensive to buy and special low-interest loans made available by the Agricultural Bank of Greece have brought them within the reach of many Cretan farmers.

The bus services are organised separately within the four Nomoi—administrative regions—each of which has its own KTEL, or bus company. Each KTEL has its own number, by which its buses may be recognised: 35, Khania; 36, Rethymnon; 37, Iraklion; 38, Lassithi. A fifth company, known as the 8th KTEYL of Crete, operates the principal inter-city services, including the expresses along the north coast highway. Under the supervision of the Ministry of Transport, the members of the KTEYL and of each KTEL settle which routes are to be operated and by whom, and what fares are to be charged. Most of the KTEL routes run to the principal town of the Nomos (region) from the outlying villages and smaller towns. Iraklion and Khania are the two main centres of attraction, both overshadowing Rethymnon lying between them. In the Nomos of Lassithi, each of the four main towns of Ayios Nikolaos, Neapolis, Ierapetra and Sitia acts as a focal point for public transport from the surrounding villages, but there is still considerable through traffic westwards to Iraklion. In addition to the four KTELs, there are separately organised town bus services in the cities of Iraklion and Khania.

Notes for motorists

Signposting has lagged behind road-building; place-names are not regularly displayed, and directional signs are by no means as frequent as the mapless motorist might wish. On new roads, signs indicating hazards, such as bends, falling rocks and so on, are frequent, but signs warning of animals on the road are rare, although the likelihood of finding them is great. After a short while, however, the visitor adjusts and begins to feel that other countries possibly have too many road signs. There is one set of traffic lights in the centre of Iraklion, but a policeman still urges on the traffic there.

All archaeological sites and most other points of interest have adequate parking places and nowhere are there unreasonable restrictions on parking. Motorists are warned not to leave a private car in a taxi park, or in an area reserved for buses. To do so is not only a traffic offence, but an infringement of the Greek sense of order.

5 PREHISTORY

IN a consideration of the prehistory of Crete three names come at once to mind: two from before the beginnings of written history and the third almost from our own time. Minos, the king, friend of mighty Zeus, is one; Knossos, where his palace stood, the second; Sir Arthur Evans, whose scholarship and archaeological skill gave the world the story of the palace, is the third. In Knossos, foremost of the Cretan palaces, we see the majesty of kingship, the social life of a royal court, and supporting them the whole infrastructure, ruled by priests, storemen, smiths and clerks. It is a measure of Evans's greatness that those who see the palace now are made aware of it as a place of power, the centre of a former realm. Reality confronts them in the wide and shining courts above and in the dim-lit halls below. Men and women lived and were made and broken here. To have left such a memorial to his work would alone be cause for fame, but Evans's *The Palace of Minos* stands as one of the great archaeological publications of the world.

THE STONE AGE

It is uncertain whether or not men of the Palaeolithic (Old Stone Age) existed in Crete, since no firm conclusion can be drawn from the single stone scraper found by Pendlebury in Lassithi nor from the obsidian microliths found in Franchet's site west of Iraklion. It must be assumed that the earliest Neolithic (New Stone Age) culture in Crete did not develop within the island but was brought from outside. Neolithic pottery and artefacts have been found in almost every part of

CRETE

Crete, but only the material from the Neolithic site at Knossos has been studied in detail. Here, Sinclair Hood makes out a good case for the inhabitants of the earliest Neolithic level excavated at Knossos not having made or used pottery, which appears for the first time for certain in the level above. The pottery found there is of a remarkably evolved type which, as Hood (1971) remarks, 'looks as if it was the heir of a long tradition' and may have come from Anatolia. Some Neolithic figurines of stone and clay are found, mostly female. Hood suggests that these do not represent gods or goddesses but are dolls, used either as playthings or in sympathetic magic. Two late Neolithic houses uncovered in the central court of the palace reveal a ground-plan in which rooms seem to have been added at random. This is a characteristic which continued in Minoan building, leading Hutchinson (1962) to observe that 'considerable ingenuity and architectural skill might be displayed in the design of individual parts of a building, but there was always an opportunist air about a Minoan building as a whole'.

THE MINOAN AGE

This is the name given by Sir Arthur Evans to the time between the end of the Neolithic and the beginning of the Iron Age in Crete. Basing his chronology upon parallel developments in Egypt and Mesopotamia, Evans divided the Minoan Age into three periods, which he called Early, Middle and Late Minoan, each having three main sub-periods. The overall time-span of the Minoan era, and the dates of transition within it from one period and sub-period to the next are subject to much discussion amongst archaeologists and to periodic revision. The dates used here are shown in Table 3 and are derived principally from Hutchinson.

5 The countryside around the ruins of Knossos

6 The Palace of Minos, Knossos: *(above)* a staircase leading to lower level ceremonial apartments; *(below)* one of the many rows of gigantic storage jars

PREHISTORY

Table 3

MINOAN CHRONOLOGY
(EM, MM and LM: Early, Middle and Late Minoan)

Hutchinson			Palmer
5500 BC	Beginning of Neolithic		
3000	EM I		
2600	EM II		
2300	EM III		
2000	MM Ia		
1900	MM Ib		
1850	MM IIa		
1780	MM IIb		
1750	MM IIIa		
1600	MM IIIb		1700
1550	LM Ia	LM Ia	1600
1500	LM Ib	LM Ib	1500
1450	LM II	LM II	1450
1420	LM III	LM III	1400
1050	Dorian invasion		1100

Sources: Hutchinson, R. W. *Prehistoric Crete* (1962, revised 1968)
Palmer, L. R. *Myceneans and Minoans*, 2nd ed (1965)

EARLY MINOAN

Early Minoan I ran from about 3000 BC to 2600 BC. The Cretans were then essentially a Neolithic people, continuing to use stone tools, and distinguished from their forebears chiefly by the higher proportion of new foreign design elements in their pottery. It is possible that copper tools and copper-working techniques might have been introduced during this period, but the first clear evidence of copper-working in Crete belongs to the Early Minoan II period.

In the second Early Minoan period (EM II) a copper-working culture developed rapidly in the Messara and in the eastern part of Crete, and more slowly elsewhere in the island. Surviving metal tools and weapons of this period are scarce, and derive

CRETE

principally from Mokhlos and other sites in eastern Crete. More common finds are personal and household items, such as jewellery and vases, made from a variety of materials and showing Anatolian, Syrian, Egyptian and Libyan influences. Stamp seals, for example, were introduced to Crete from Anatolia and Syria, the first to be made in Crete being fashioned from Syrian ivory and Cretan steatite (soapstone). Many fine vases were also made, some from local stone and some from imported materials, such as obsidian. The shape of the vase was roughed out with a copper drill used with an abrasive dust and then finished by grinding. Egyptian shapes are sometimes found, but the more exotic forms are from Asia Minor.

Material of this type has been excavated from settlement sites such as the so-called 'House on the Hill' at Vasilikí, a miniature forerunner of the great palaces of Knossos, Phaistos, Mallia and Zakros and also from various burial sites. The most famous of the burial sites are the round tombs of the Messara; these first appear in EM II, and their use continued for generations. They are free-standing stone-built structures, not with vaulted roofs of stone, as Xanthoudídis (1924) originally thought, but, if roofed at all, covered with timber or thatch. They are thus very different from the chamber tombs of Mycenae, and were thought by Evans and Pendlebury to provide further evidence of Libyan and Egyptian influence upon Crete.

The transition from EM II to EM III occurs about 2300 BC, although both periods have many common features. For example, EM III tombs are not distinguishable by their architecture from those of the preceding period and, indeed, many EM II tombs, both stone-built and in caves, continued in use throughout EM III into MM I. Seals of EM III are numerous and greatly varied in design. Egyptian motifs are sufficiently frequent to indicate direct contact between Egypt and the Messara, where seals of Cretan workmanship are found along with Egyptian imports. In the north, Knossos and other settlements appear to have had well-developed trading relations with the Cyclades.

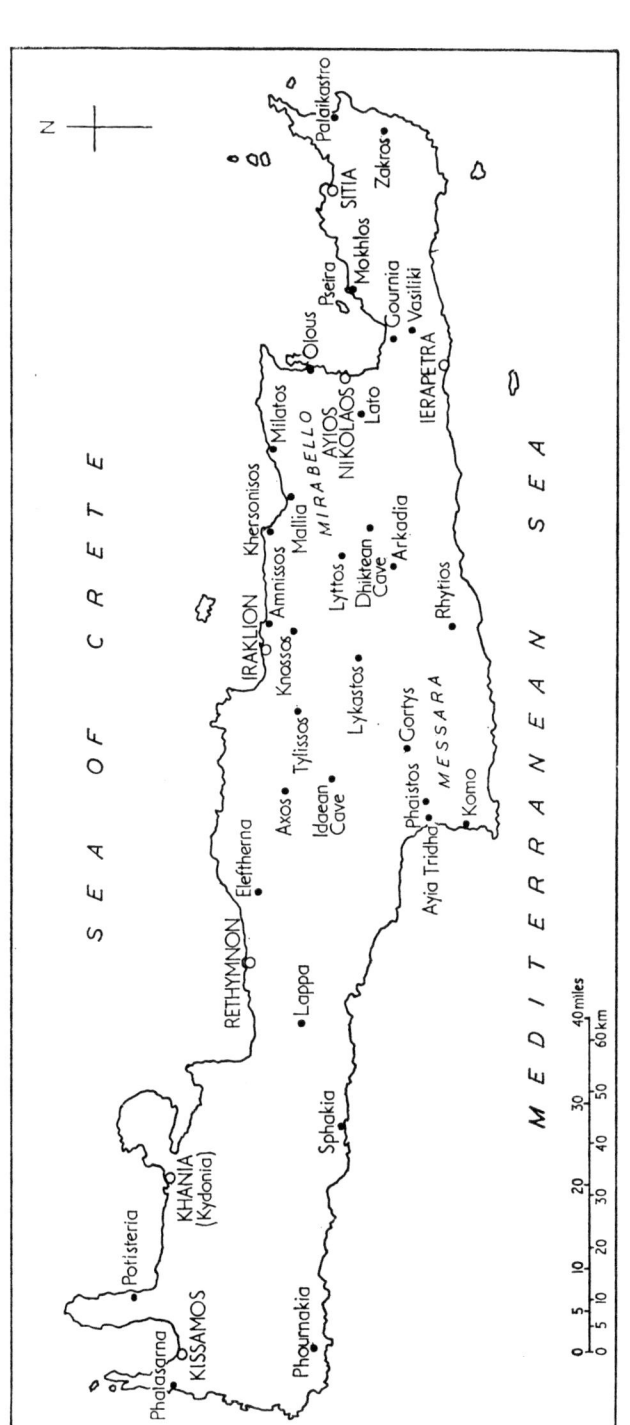

Main archaeological sites

CRETE

During the three phases of the Early Minoan period some clearly marked social changes were taking place. The population of Crete increased rapidly; in the east of the island immigrants came from Asia Minor to Palaikastro, Pseíra, Mokhlos and Gournia, and in the Messara there is evidence of new arrivals from Libya who settled at many places in the plain. The architecture of private houses advanced greatly, but without any corresponding development in the art of planning. For the first time the population began to leave the open country and to concentrate in villages and towns, and the purely pastoral society declined. Instead of each family making what it needed in wood, pottery and metal, the crafts became specialised; men whom Homer called '*demioergoi*'—literally 'men who work for the people'—set up as specialists, and professionalism in craft and art was born.

MIDDLE MINOAN

The 'urban revolution' which had begun during the Early Minoan period was gaining momentum at the end of EM III and sweeping through Crete. The importance to Europe of this change in the way of life of the Cretans is that, in Hutchinson's words, it 'provided a channel through which flowed the cultural products and influences of the older civilisations of Mesopotamia, Syria, Anatolia and Egypt into the less developed lands of Europe'. The study of the great Minoan works of art and of the great buildings of the Cretan kings is a worthy one by any standard, but it has a particular significance for all who live under the laws and customs of the western world.

The facts of the beginning of urban life in Crete and its far-reaching effects are clear enough, at least in outline, but the immediate causes are not yet established. Influence from outside Crete is possible—the pre-pottery city wall of Jericho provides evidence of early urbanisation in the Eastern Mediterranean basin. The rapid increase of population during the Early Minoan period together with the arrival of more skilled farmers from Asia Minor and Libya would have led to an in-

PREHISTORY

crease in agricultural production and possibly to increased general prosperity. One skill almost certainly brought to Crete by the men of Libya and Asia Minor was that of irrigation, which is known to have been developed in Mycenean society to the point of being a public service. The water-bailiff in *Iliad* XXI 257 is a man with official standing.

There is also evidence that great improvements in transport took place early in the first Middle Minoan period. Pendlebury (1939) speaks of the 'regularisation of the great route across the island from Komo in the south to Knossos'. It has also been suggested by Gordon Childe that wheeled transport, built in the form of waggons and carts with no steering, was introduced to Crete in about 2000 BC. Although primitive, such vehicles would be a great advance over pack animals for farm transport even if they could only be used on the flat. A model of one such waggon dated to MM I was found at Palaikastro in eastern Crete. Such changes as these, when allied to the gregarious nature of Mediterranean peoples, and to the centralisation inseparable from government, could account for the growth of towns and cities in the Middle Minoan period.

A striking parallel may be drawn between these developments in the Middle Minoan period and similar changes which have taken place in Crete since about 1960. There have been dramatic alterations in agricultural practice, the first since Roman times; irrigation has been extended to new areas, every village has been made accessible by motor road, and motorised transport is in general use. Hence surplus agricultural workers are migrating to the urban centres in search of new kinds of work, while those who remain on the land have easy access to the attractions and facilities of the large towns.

During the Middle Minoan period the island's commercial and cultural centre of gravity shifted from the east to the centre; the change is reflected in the building of the great palaces of central Crete: Knossos, Mallia, Phaistos and Ayia Triádha. At Knossos and Phaistos, the EM strata were cut away to clear the sites for the foundations of the MM I palaces, so that in the

CRETE

central court at Knossos and in several parts of the palace of Phaistos late Neolithic buildings are found directly beneath the MM I paving. The earlier palace of Mallia also dates from MM I and seems to have been planned as a unity and to have survived with some changes into MM III. The situation at Knossos and Phaistos is more obscure because neither palace was built to a systematic plan, and both were laid in ruins by an earthquake in 1730 BC during MM IIb. The Cretans of the Messara appear to have recovered from this catastrophe more quickly than the Knossians, and at Phaistos an even more magnificent palace rose from the ruins of the old. This was later destroyed by another earthquake sometime in MM III. A new palace was also built on the seaward end of the same ridge. This palace takes its modern name of Ayia Triadha from the neighbouring medieval chapel of the Holy Trinity, for its ancient name is unknown. As a place to live, Ayia Triadha has advantages over Phaistos. Its climate is more pleasant—when Phaistos is burning in the heat reflected from the Messara, over which it commands a wide and splendid view, Ayia Triadha has freshness from the sea and even the summer nights are cool. The site would have been less easy to defend than the steeper Phaistos, but neither palace was fortified,

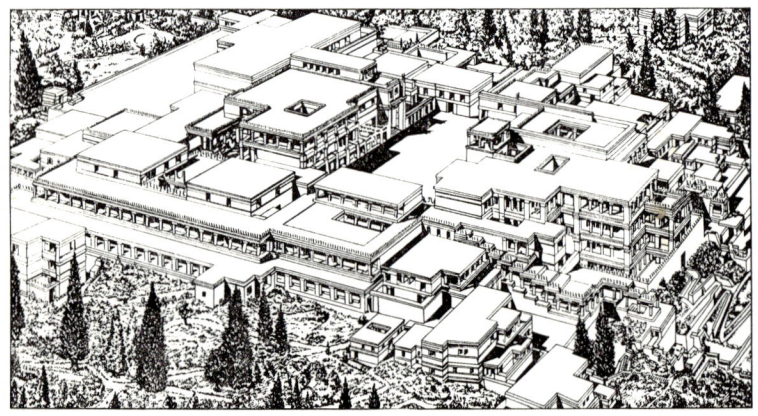

Knossos: a conjectural reconstruction of the Palace of Minos

PREHISTORY

and their rulers clearly expected no attack from land or sea.

The lack of defensive features even in those Minoan palaces close to the sea shows that no attackers were feared. This has been held to prove that the Minoan kings had navies which ruled the Aegean, if not the whole of the eastern Mediterranean. Vessels faster than the merchant ships and filled with armed men could have been used against pirates, but the real protection came from the intelligence gathered by the countless merchantmen whose trade routes radiated out from Crete across the Aegean and the Libyan seas. Thus, with a large volume of Minoan shipping calling at foreign ports and crisscrossing the seas round Crete, the island would have been safe from any large-scale surprise attack, and could have enjoyed peace and security as a spin-off from its predominance in foreign trade. This is not the same as a maritime supremacy based on a fleet of warships, which some scholars have considered to be impossible.

Cultural advances

Life as lived in the great palaces of Crete was the life of an affluent society which wanted for nothing and could call on measureless resources of wealth and on superb craftsmanship and exquisite artistry. Every need and comfort in daily life was supplied, and no pains or expense were spared to make the environment worthy of the rich and happy beings who were cocooned within it. The palaces had wide courts, and their rooms were decorated with paintings and sculptures of great beauty. Objects of domestic and ceremonial use were exquisitely adorned with abstract and naturalistic designs of flowers, animals and sea creatures. Like the wall-paintings, the skilful designs, some relaxed, others vibrant with life, reflect in their clear colours and flowing lines the delight of their makers. The fragments of this beauty which survive today can offer us only a little of the feelings of pleasure which they must have brought to those who used and made them.

In order to achieve the production of these masterpieces,

CRETE

advances had been made in most aspects of basic technology. In MM I, most metal objects were made of copper, but some were of bronze, an alloy of copper and tin harder than either pure metal. By MM III, however, substantially all weapons and tools were of bronze. The goldsmiths' work of this period is also of a new excellence, perhaps connected with improved tools. The outstanding example is the hornet pendant from the ossuary of Khrysólakkos—the Gold Hole—at Mallia. This superb piece, which escaped the looters throughout the centuries, shows most of the metal-working techniques in use at the time. These include casting, wire-drawing, welding, drilling and punching, engraving, filigree and a delicate use of granulation.

At Knossos, the art of faïence reached its full development; surviving examples include decorated plaques and the famous figurine of the Snake Goddess, with her bare breasts and long flounced skirt. From the number of engraved seal stones which have survived, it would seem as if every MM III citizen had his own personal seal. These stones are in many designs and are made from many materials, some very hard and none easy to work on a miniature scale; among them are cornelian, steatite, chalcedony, haematite, greenstone, agate and onyx.

Nor in this period were splendour and luxury restricted to the palaces. Opulent and lavishly decorated mansions were built in the towns, and in the countryside magnificent villas were built both as residences for the great farmers and as country houses for the urban aristocracy.

Cretan hieroglyphic scripts

A further important aspect of life in the Middle Minoan period was the use of a locally developed hieroglyphic script. Examples have been found engraved on numerous seal stones, and inscribed on large stones and clay tablets. The history of the development of the script goes back some 600 years before the beginning of MM, into the Early Minoan period. In EM I seals with pictographic designs are rare, and those that do exist cannot be accurately dated. However, in EM II engraved seals

PREHISTORY

begin to be found in stratified deposits at Mokhlos and Sphoungarás; these suggest an Egyptian origin and appear to be merely signs of ownership with no specific meaning as texts. By EM III a native Cretan hieroglyphic script had begun to develop, which owed some of its symbols to Egypt, but was in the main independent. Many of these seals bear only a single design, which is the device or sign-manual of their owner, whereas in MM I many seals were made having hieroglyphic inscriptions of several symbols. The seal stones are usually long triangular prisms cut in steatite or in some other soft stone, but some four-sided examples also occur. Evans called this script Hieroglyphic Script A, and a later development of it Hieroglyphic Script B. Both scripts together contain 135 signs, of which 42 are found in Script A only and 44 in Script B only, with 49 signs common to both A and B. The hieroglyphs of Script A are easy to recognise as pictures of common objects, such as a sitting or walking man, a jug, or a ship; some depict animals, such as wolves and horned sheep, which are no longer found in Crete. Evans considered that most of the hieroglyphs were of local invention, although he admitted that some, including the ship, could have had Egyptian origins. The rigging of these ships is like that of the Egyptian and Phoenician ships, with a large central square sail, but the hull differs in having a high prow and a long low stern. The pictures in Hieroglyphic Script A were usually hollowed out or had raised outlines, sometimes with internal detail, but those in Hieroglyphic Script B were mere outlines, suggesting that they would soon develop into a non-pictorial linear script. Script B hieroglyphic seals began at Knossos in MM II, and by MM IIb and MM III were of excellent workmanship and often cut on hard stones, such as agate (found in the Mirabello Eparchy), rock crystal and jasper. Where, however, contemporary inscriptions are found on clay, the designs start to become conventional rather than representational, thus suggesting that they were beginning to stand for sounds. When this process is complete, the script has developed into a syllabary.

CRETE

Linear A

It was thought by Evans and others that during MM IIIa Linear A evolved in Crete from Hieroglyphic Script B. However, Professor Levi's more recent excavations at Phaistos have brought to light new evidence, in the form of tablets written in a script transitional to Linear A, suggesting that Linear A itself was in use as early as 1850 BC, that is, in MM IIa. Its use apparently did not spread to northern Crete and to Knossos for over a century. The people of Mallia, who seem always to have lagged behind the rest of central Crete in the adoption of the latest scripts, only began to use Linear A in MM IIIb.

This script, the first of the Cretan true syllabaries to be found in any quantity and over a large area, has not been deciphered or translated. This leaves us without any clue to the language in which it is written, and the circumstances in which the script itself was developed remain lamentably obscure. The archaeological evidence has been variously interpreted. Some still regard Linear A, in the Evans tradition, as a purely Cretan script developed initially at Phaistos somewhat earlier than had previously been thought. Others suggest that it represents either a local Cretan language written in an imported script or that both language and script were imported.

The Phaistos disk

This famous but puzzling object was found in a clay container in a room in the Palace of Phaistos, along with some MM IIIb vases and a tablet inscribed in Linear A. The disk is of clay, 16cm (6·3in) in diameter, impressed before baking with symbols running spirally on both sides from the rim to the centre. Each character was impressed separately with a stamp, and none of them has any resemblance to the Minoan hieroglyphs. The human figures are not Minoan, and it is now generally thought that the disk was brought to Crete from Anatolia. Although various bold but improbable attempts have been made, no acceptable decipherment or translation has yet

PREHISTORY

resulted. The disk, whatever it is, was certainly an anachronism in Phaistos in the seventeenth century BC.

LATE MINOAN

Since Evans first worked out and presented to the world the broad spectrum of Minoan chronology, a great step has been taken towards clarifying the relation of its concluding phases with events in the rest of the Mediterranean, and towards a fuller understanding of the internal history of Crete itself as related to the archaeological finds. In particular, new light has been shed on the LM period, but it is not yet possible to unravel with certainty many of the tangled threads of evidence—almost as many new questions have been posed as old ones answered. It has, however, become clear that Minoan chronology in the future will owe much to the evidence provided for the decipherment of Linear B by Ventris and Chadwick, and that archaeologists will be aided by the information extracted from texts written in that script.

Linear B

It should first be said that the affluent society of MM III continued on into the LM period with only minor changes in life style. During LM I palace administrative records continued to be written in Linear A. The script called Linear B superseded Linear A at Knossos at a date given by Evans as 1450 BC (LM II). This date, although defended by others, is not accepted by Palmer (1965) who on the evidence developed in his book prefers a date nearer 1300 BC (end of LM III). This also is hotly disputed. On present evidence, Linear B has not been found elsewhere in Crete, but was in use in several places on the mainland of Greece. Inscribed vessels were found at Mycenae and at various other Mycenean sites such as Thebes, Tiryns and Orchomenos. Early finds of this kind were dismissed as imports from Knossos until, in 1939, Professor Carl Blegen (1955), when digging at Pylos, in the western Peloponnese, found 600 Linear B tablets in the 'Archives Room' of Nestor's palace.

CRETE

This discovery, somewhat difficult to explain away in terms of trade, severely jolted the traditional assumption that Late Minoan civilisation was of purely Cretan and Eastern origin, and not influenced by Greece. This led to a focusing of attention on Linear B in the hope that its decipherment might provide a key to the problem.

Work in the field was interrupted by World War II, but many scholars continued to devote time and thought to the study of the script. In 1948, Alice J. Kober drew attention to the possibility that Linear B represented an inflected language, with unchanging signs for the roots of words, followed by a series of others for the changing terminations. Michael Ventris had for some time been working on the Minoan scripts using the techniques of code and cipher breaking, in which he was highly skilled. He had already identified a number of Cretan place-names, and these, together with Miss Kober's work, led him in the early 1950s to the realisation that the inflections of Linear B were Greek inflections, resembling quite closely those of Homeric Greek. Thus he was able to identify many of the Linear B groups as Greek words with known meanings, although he had previously thought that the language of the tablets was not Greek. The scientific decipherment of Linear B by this method is the first time that the key to an unknown script has been discovered without the assistance of a bilingual text. It is unfortunate that Ventris died soon after the publication of his first results and that he could not take his own part in the fierce controversy which his work aroused. However, his fellow-worker John Chadwick (1958) and others have continued to apply the technique to the Linear B documents. Some archaeologists refused absolutely to accept Ventris's interpretation of Linear B as Greek; others did accept it; while others attempted to ignore his work altogether.

The whole idea that the Myceneans spoke Greek and that they introduced the language to Crete was so startling as to be instinctively unacceptable to many, and it is only with the passing of time and the re-sifting of other evidence that the theory has reached the stage of being considered respectable. Professor Palmer has done a great deal to correlate the deductions to be made from the tablets with the evidence from Cretan and Mycenean pottery. He reconsidered the evidence of the stirrup-jars, for example. These are distinctively shaped jars used in the storage and transport of 'unguents'—olive oil rendered aromatic by boiling with herbs and spices, such as coriander, sesame, white safflower, fennel, pennyroyal, cumin and mint. Jars of this type, some with their seals unbroken and many bearing Linear B inscriptions, have been found at a large number of sites associated with Mycenean expansion on the mainland of Greece and in the islands. Stirrup-jars only became common at Knossos at the very end of LM II. At this time, the palaces of Crete suffered widespread destruction by an unknown cause which was thought by Evans, who rejected the idea of an invasion, to have been a natural disaster of some kind. This was obviously of a more horrifying and drastic nature than the earthquakes with which the palace-builders were so familiar.

The rebuilding of the palaces at the beginning of LM II was accompanied by the appearance at Knossos of Linear B texts written in Greek. At the same time, stirrup-jars first became plentiful in Crete. Thus there is archaeological evidence to suggest that in LM III the occupants of the rebuilt Palace of Minos were Greek-speaking Myceneans or, as Homer calls them, Achaeans. In political terms, it is far from surprising that the power vacuum left by the widespread destruction in Crete should have appealed to the predatory and opportunist instincts of the imperialistic Myceneans.

The eruption of Thira

The theory that Minoan civilisation was destroyed in about 1400 BC by a severe eruption of the volcano of Thira or Santorini, the ancient Kallísti, was first put forward by Professor Marinatos in 1939. It is only in recent years, however, that it has received popular notice and support outside Greece.

The present island of Thira, or Santorini, its associated islet

CRETE

of Thirasía and the small active cone of Néa Kaiméni, rising from the sea almost in the centre of the circular harbour, are virtually all that is now left of the original great volcano. Thus Thira today forms what vulcanologists call a caldera, that is, the large crater or hollow remaining when the upper part of a conical volcano has been blown away. Since the caldera of Thira is the largest of its kind in the world, it is reasonable to assume that the eruption must have been of huge power. In the absence of documentary evidence, Professor Marinatos turned to the 1883 eruption of Krakatau in Indonesia to provide a model of the possibilities.

The relative scales of the two events may be seen by comparing the amount of land which sank or was blown away in each case: at Thira an estimated 83 square kilometres disappeared, at Krakatau only 22·8 square kilometres. Krakatau island was covered by 20 metres of pumice, while on Thira a depth of 30 metres still remains after more than three millennia of erosion. The blast from the explosions of Krakatau on 27 August 1883 broke windows and blew down walls at places 200 kilometres distant. Volcanic bombs were thrown to a distance of 80 kilometres and clouds of volcanic dust or tephra turned day into night over a radius of 200 kilometres. Spectacular as they were, these aspects of the eruption were far exceeded in destructive power by the great sea waves that swept out from the exploding island volcano. They reached the nearby coasts of Sumatra and Java with a height of 30 metres, and at Tcloek-Bctoeng, 90 kilometres from Krakatau, the steamship *Barouw* was plucked from the harbour and carried over the town, finishing up in a forest 3 kilometres inland.

Professor Marinatos has developed his theory of the destruction of Cretan civilisation with great ingenuity, but certain fundamental questions must be answered before it can be accepted in its present form. When precisely did the eruption take place? Were its effects serious enough to destroy Minoan civilisation either directly by volcanic bombs and tidal waves or indirectly by spreading such a pall of ash and pumice over

PREHISTORY

the countryside that vegetation could not survive? Much interdisciplinary effort is being put into answering these questions. Excavations are continuing on Thira to obtain more chronological data. A further dimension of uncertainty has been introduced with respect to Crete by the discovery that pumice from Thira, found in levels dated from 1500 BC to 1400 BC at a Bronze Age site at Nichoria in the western Peloponnese, had been carried there by human agency in sufficient quantity for use in some domestic or industrial process. The excavators took particular note that pumice was not found before 1500 BC, and that it became much less plentiful after about 1400 BC. This discovery makes it possible that the relatively small amount of pumice found at Mallia was not, as had been assumed by some scholars, directly deposited by the eruption of Thira, but was transported and stored there for use as an abrasive or for some other purpose.

CRETE UNDER THE MYCENEANS

From 1400 to 1200 BC, Crete was ruled from the Greek mainland by the Myceneans. There was probably a colony at Knossos which ruled directly over the other cities, perhaps over all those listed in the *Homeric Catalogue of Ships*: 'the walled town of Gortys, Lyktos and Miletus, and shining white Lykastos, Phaistos and Rhytios, cities fair'. Hutchinson suggests that only Knossos and its neighbouring cities were ruled by the Myceneans, and that the land of the Eteocretans, east of Sitia, remained for a time independent. The distribution of known sites of the period is denser in the centre and east of the island, with only a few west of Rethymnon, such as Sphakiá, Khania (Kydónia), Potistéria and Phournákia. It seems likely that the comparative paucity of identified sites may be due to the fact that they have yet to be found, since archaeological effort has been concentrated in the eastern and central parts of the island. Recent work in the neighbourhood of Khania is revealing sites which go back to Mycenean times and beyond.

CRETE

The architectural remains of the period are typically Mycenean. The most striking innovation is the readily recognisable *megaron*, or standard royal palace, introduced at this time from the mainland, and consisting in general of a porch or forecourt, an antechamber, and a great hall for the men and women's quarters, with a passage along one side. The *megaron* at Ayia Triadha is in four sections and built on top of the old Minoan palace. At Tylissos there is one almost as large, found by Dr Platon, and a good example at Zakros in eastern Crete. Knossos itself provides evidence of a *megaron* within the Minoan palace area, associated with undisturbed Linear B tablets. The discovery was made by Evans on the third day of his excavation, 31 March 1900, and the facts of it have been much obscured by the efforts of later scholars and indeed of Evans himself to bring them within the framework of established thought. In the light of present knowledge, however, the interpretation of what Evans found that day is clear: it is a *megaron* like those of Ayia Triadha, Tylissos and sandy Pýlos.

The social and political history of Crete under the Myceneans is still being written. The social organisation is well set out by Palmer. The head of state is the king, *wanax*; the army is commanded by the *lawagetas*; then there is the warrior class, *telestai*, who served in war in return for a holding of land. There is a separate class of priests, called *hierewes*, and a class of craftsmen or *demiowergoi*, which included professional men. Homer includes in this second group the prophet, the healer of diseases, the craftsmen in timber, and the herald. Finally there are the slaves, *douloi*. This organisation is based upon the evidence obtained from Linear B tablets, which are largely business documents. No reference is made to the existence of tribes, *phylai*, or brotherhoods, *phratriai*: both important social groupings belonging to long-established custom, to religion, and to traditional law. With the addition of the tribes and brotherhoods, however, there is a very close resemblance between Mycenean social organisation and that of the later Dorian cities of Crete from 700 to 400 BC. Detailed evidence of Dorian

7 Iraklion: *(above)* the Venetian fort and inner harbour, now reserved for small craft; *(below)* the Morosini fountain in the old town centre – one of the relatively few surviving Venetian monuments

8 Iraklion: *(above)* the inner harbour, with the Koule or Venetian fort. The new harbour is to the right; *(below)* the street market

PREHISTORY

social structure is available from a contemporary—fifth century BC—inscription: the great Laws of Gortys (see p 90).

CRETE UNDER THE DORIANS

The Myceneans were driven from Crete, and a little later from Mycenae itself, by another wave of conquerors whom it is convenient to call Dorians, although controversy about their origin has raged for many years. The Greek quality of Crete, dating back to the first arrival of the Myceneans, was strengthened by the Dorians who were also Greeks. Later centuries of occupation and oppression by Romans, Arabs, Venetians, Turks and Germans did not succeed in obliterating the essential character of the Cretans. Some would like to attribute this ethnic persistence to the Dorians, but unfortunately there is no evidence. After the coming of the Dorians, Crete receded from the international scene, and the Cretans lived unremarkable but apparently prosperous lives in their own cities.

The remoteness of Crete from the main stream of Greek life and culture in the first half of the fifth century BC is emphasised by Pindar in the twelfth Olympian, which celebrates the victory of one Ergoteles in the long foot-race at Olympia. If he had stayed at home in Knossos, says Pindar, instead of emigrating to Sicily, no one would ever have heard of him and he would have been like a farmyard rooster, famous on his own dunghill, and that only for a season.

The cities had enough resources to indulge in wars between themselves, and some had ties with cities on the mainland. The population was at a high enough level for many of the men to take military service abroad. Cretan mercenaries, particularly archers and slingers, were famous throughout antiquity until Roman times. The pattern of settlement remained much the same throughout the island as it had been since the 'urban revolution' of Middle Minoan times.

CRETE

The Laws of Gortys
The cities of Crete played a great part in the development and codification of civil law, and the Cretans were much admired as authorities in the fields of jurisprudence and political philosophy throughout classical times. The earliest written legal document in Europe is the great inscription of the Laws of Gortys. Its text dates from the first half of the fifth century BC and some of the material in it is still earlier (Willetts, 1968). The first inscribed stone of the Laws to be found was discovered in 1857 in the wall of a water-mill near the ruined church of St Titus at Gortys. The significance of this fragment was not established until 1878, and in 1879 a similar fragment was seen in a house nearby and its text was copied. No more was found until Federigo Halbherr visited the mill in 1884 and saw some inscribed stones when the water-level in the channel was low. He was able to copy four columns of the text, but the landowner would not let him follow the course of the wall into the adjacent field. On his return to Iraklion, Halbherr told Ernst Fabricius of the German Institute at Athens what he had seen and showed him the copy. Fabricius, when he visited the site in October, had more success with the landowner and dug a trench as far as the end of the inscription.

It could be seen that the blocks bearing the inscription, of which twelve columns are preserved, once formed part of a *tholos*, or circular building, some 30 metres (98ft) in diameter, with the inscribed surface facing inwards. This building has entirely disappeared, and the blocks of the inscription owe their preservation to the fact that in the first century BC or thereabouts they were built into a roughly semi-circular wall behind the stage of a Roman theatre. When removed from their original position in the *tholos*, the stones were numbered so that they could be re-erected in the right order. The form of these numbers indicates the approximate date of the re-use of the stones. The inscription is written in twelve columns, each originally five blocks high, of which four now remain. Each

PREHISTORY

column is about 1½ metres (5ft) high and there are 53 to 56 lines of writing, the height of individual letters being about 2½cm (1in).

The text consists of a series of laws relating to citizenship, marriage, tenure of property and inheritance. Each pronouncement is in the form 'If such and such happens, then the legal position is that . . .' The property rights of married and divorced women are clearly set out. A wife's dowry and inheritance remained subject to her control and could not be sold or used as security by her husband. Divorce was a right of married couples, at the instigation of either party, and seems to have been common. A divorced wife could, if the husband had been the cause of the divorce, claim back any property which she had brought to her husband, together with half the produce from her own property—she had to pay her husband for anything else that she took.

The law regarded the safeguarding of property interests as of paramount importance. The rights of serfs and slaves were carefully defined, as were the rights of a man who gave himself in bondage for debt. Inheritance rights in cases of adoption were defined: an adopted son could become sole heir if there were no legitimate sons; otherwise the adopted son took a daughter's share. The division of the population into age-groups, before and after puberty, and the age for full citizenship was laid down, and regulations were promulgated for the membership of the Dorian tribes and of the brotherhoods.

The Laws distinguish sharply between social classes, as can be seen from the variation in the fines by which certain offences were punished. The credence given to witnesses varied with their social status, the evidence of only free men being accepted in some cases. The privileged classes were favoured throughout. In cases of rape, for example, the fine levied is far heavier for the rape of a free woman than for that of a serf, which in turn is greater than for that of a slave. Most offences are punishable by fines or by restitution and no barbaric penalties are mentioned. The Laws contain no mention of the death penalty.

6 CRETE UNDER THE ROMANS, THE ARABS AND BYZANTIUM

ROMAN CONQUEST AND OCCUPATION

SINCE the end of the third century BC, Rome had for reasons of policy been induced to intervene in increasing strength in the Eastern Mediterranean. After over a century of intermittent warfare, Macedonia became a Roman province in 168 BC. When Greece was later annexed to Macedonia in 146 BC, the whole of the Greek peninsula came directly under Roman control. At this time the island of Crete was still free, and remained so for a further seventy-nine years. Rome's next involvement in the East was with Mithridates of Pontus whose dominions lay to the east of the Dardanelles on the southern shore of the Black Sea. Between 87 and 67 BC the Romans waged three wars against him. The cities of Crete, in particular Knossos, had long had close ties with the kingdom of Pontus and, although Roman diplomacy was strong enough to prevent a formal alliance, Mithridates's ambassadors were received with favour and the Cretans sent troops to fight against the Romans. In addition, the harbours of Crete were always open to Mithridates's ships when seeking refuge from bad weather or from Roman pursuit.

Inconvenienced by this policy, the Romans finally declared war on Crete with the object of subduing the island. This war was separate and distinct from the operations already being conducted by Gnaeus Pompeius Magnus against the Mediterranean pirates, who had many bases in Crete.

The first Roman attack on Crete was made by the Praetor

CRETE UNDER ROMANS, ARABS, BYZANTIUM

Marcus Antonius in 72 BC. Defeated at sea by the Cretan admirals Panares and Lasthenes, he was compelled to make peace on terms humiliating to Rome. After diplomatic overtures for the subjection of the island had failed, the Proconsul Quintus Caecilius Metellus was sent with three legions in 69 BC to take possession of the island. The Cretans faced him near Kydonia (Khania), but his superior force caused them to retreat. The war then became a series of sieges of Cretan cities. Kydonia, Knossos, Lyttos, Eleftherna and Lappa fell in turn after resisting desperately. At this moment Octavius, Pompey's second-in-command, was invited by the Cretans to intervene, since they thought that they would obtain better terms from him than from Mettellus, who was carrying out a scorched earth policy. Octavius's intervention angered Mettellus and moved him to even greater excesses of savagery. His brutality to prisoners became such that many garrisons preferred suicide to surrender. All resistance in Crete came to an end in 67 BC when the Cretan general Aristion surrendered Ierapetra.

Thus Crete became a Roman province. It was, according to some authorities, at first joined to Cyrene although it is known that the two provinces were separate in 44 BC. Augustus subsequently joined Crete to Cyrene and made them into one senatorial province under a governor of praetorian rank. This arrangement lasted until the reign of Diocletian (AD 284–305) when Crete again became a separate province.

After the conquest of 67 BC, Crete enjoyed a long peace lasting, with few disturbances, until the island was first overrun by the Arabs in AD 651. The Roman peace put an end to the internecine strife between the cities of Crete and, owing to its position on the main Roman trade routes between East and West, the island not only became extremely prosperous but absorbed a great deal more of Roman culture and customs than did the Greek mainland. Gortys, the Roman capital of Crete, had several hundred thousand inhabitants and Strabo says that the city measured 50 *stadia* (9·5 kilometres) across. Christopher Buondelmonti, a visitor to this site at the beginning of the

CRETE

fifteenth century, was astonished to see thousands of broken statues and fallen architectural members. Many of the statues are now in the archaeological museum at Iraklion, but the activities of Venetian governors and, in more recent times, of souvenir hunters and antique dealers, have scattered many others in museums and private houses throughout Europe and America.

THE ARABS IN CRETE

After the dissolution of the Roman Empire under Constantine the Great, Crete came peacefully under the rule of the Eastern Roman Empire. Peace continued in Crete until AD 651 when an Arab fleet plundered the island. The Arabs maintained a base for piracy there until 674 when they abandoned it and it was returned to the rule of Byzantium for a further 149 years. In 823, civil war at the heart of the Empire provided the Arabs with an opportunity to seize the outlying islands of Sicily and Crete. In the same year, Saracen Arabs from Spain, led by Emir Abū Hafs 'Umar b. 'Īsā (the Apochapsis of the Byzantine historians) plundered Crete. Next year they returned under the same Emir with forty ships and landed a large force near where Iraklion now stands. The Emir burnt his ships to ensure that his men should have no thought of abandoning this island—flowing, as he said, with milk and honey. They set up a fortress surrounded by a deep trench at a spot indicated to them, according to tradition, by a hermit. In a short time they had made themselves masters of the whole island. They called their capital Hadak; it was known to the Byzantines as Handax, and to the Venetians and Turks as Candia before it acquired its modern name of Iraklion.

Throughout the 135 years that the Arabs held Crete, Iraklion was a stronghold from which Arab pirates from Spain, Africa and Egypt ravaged the coasts and islands of Greece. A slave market was held there which supplied eastern Emirs and Egyptian potentates with the flower of Greek youth and beauty to adorn their courts and fill their harems. The Metropolitan Cyril was martyred when the Roman capital, Gortys, fell to the Arabs and his cathedral, the Church of Titus the Apostle, was destroyed. In all, nineteen cities are said to have been sacked. Only in the mountain fastness of Sphakia did a handful of Christians survive and keep their freedom.

Between AD 825 and 950, five major expeditionary forces were sent by the Byzantine Emperors to recover Crete from the Saracens. All failed because of the incompetence of the high command. The Arabs in Crete remained a painful thorn in the side of the Empire until the island was reconquered in 960 by Nicephorus Phokas. Iraklion held out throughout the winter of 960–1. An Arab expeditionary force from Asia and Africa was sent to attack the besiegers in the rear. It was intercepted by a force of Armenians which Phokas detached for this purpose after receiving intelligence reports on the Arab landing and route through Crete. In a night action the Armenians cut the enemy to pieces. Phokas announced his victory in Iraklion by loading his siege artillery with the severed heads of Arab soldiers and firing them into the city.

Two other amusing incidents—to quote a Cretan historian—occurred during the siege. One day an Arab woman of horrible appearance went up on to one of the towers of the city in view of the besiegers and called down by words and gestures the vengeance of Allah on the infidels. Finally she stripped off her clothes and put herself in a number of indelicate and revealing postures. The superstitious Byzantine soldiers, thinking she was a witch, were thrown into confusion until one of their number, cooler than the rest, shot her off her perch. Another day the Byzantine artillerymen wanted to amuse themselves at the expense of the starving Arabs in the city and fired a live donkey from a stone-throwing machine. The poor beast landed on its back in the city and lay with its legs waving in the air, causing the Byzantine troops and their commanding general to dissolve into uncontrollable laughter. Iraklion finally fell on 7 March 961. The city was ruthlessly sacked, but Nicephorus Phokas

CRETE

took the Arab commander to Constantinople where he and his family were honourably treated.

CRETE RETURNED TO THE EASTERN ROMAN EMPIRE

Under the re-established rule of Constantinople, Iraklion became the civil and religious capital of Crete. The island was ruled by a Duke of Crete who was its civil governor and supreme military commander. The Duke and his staff were chosen from the kin of the Emperor. A kind of feudalism seems to have been introduced at this time by the noble families who lived in Crete and by those who settled there. The lands belonging to these families were cultivated by a class of men called *parici*, who were christianised Arabs, and by serfs, who were prisoners of war or simply bought slaves.

The Patriarchate of Constantinople restored the church in Crete and retained the names of the bishoprics as they had been before the Arab occupation, although the former metropolitan cities had disappeared. Gortys, Knossos, Arkadia, Ierapetra, Khersonisos, Kydonia, Syvritos, Lappa and Kissamos were no more, but their bishops lived and worked in other places which often came to be called Episkopi. The Metropolitan of Gortys became Archbishop of Crete and removed to Iraklion where a cathedral church was built and dedicated, like that of Gortys, to the Apostle Titus, the patron saint of Crete. This church, a building of great splendour, remained in use throughout the Byzantine period until 1204.

The history of Crete under later Byzantine rule was uneventful, except for the seizure of the island by the rebel admiral Caryces in 1092. The Emperor Alexius I Comnenus sent John Ducas with a large fleet to deal with Caryces in Crete and another rebel, Rhapsomates, who had seized Cyprus. As soon as the Cretans heard that Ducas had reached Karpathos, they killed Caryces and surrendered Crete to the imperial forces. Alexius I later gave Crete to Diogenes Nicephorus who subsequently led a conspiracy against him. It is claimed by Xanthoudidis (1964) that one result of the rising of Caryces was the introduction of the governing of Crete by the Archontopouli: twelve men who were sent to Crete with their families and given extensive fiefs there. From them were descended the noble Cretan families who led the resistance movement throughout the period of the Venetian occupation.

7 CRETE UNDER THE VENETIANS

BY AD 1200 the Eastern Roman or Byzantine Empire, ruled from Constantinople, had so shrunk that there remained only Asia Minor, Thrace, Eastern and Central Macedonia, Thessaly, Crete and some other islands. Invaders from northern and western Europe, known generically as Franks or Latins, were in process of acquiring the mainland of Greece. In the south the Seljuk Turks held Egypt and Cyrenaica, and in the east they were pressing hard on the frontier of Asia Minor.

The two Italian states of Genoa and Venice had by this time established mercantile spheres of influence in the Eastern Mediterranean extending, in the case of Venice, as far as Alexandria. Of the two city states, it was Venice that ruled over Crete for four and a half centuries.

The story of the acquisition of Crete by Venice is contained in the involved politics of the Fourth Crusade, proclaimed by Pope Innocent in 1202. En route to the Holy Land the Crusaders diverted to Constantinople, captured it in 1204, and then set about sharing out among themselves the remnants of the Byzantine Empire. Venice, in return for providing the Crusaders with sea transport, was also to have a share. The commander-in-chief of the Crusaders, Boniface of Monferrat, was to have Crete and Asia Minor while Count Baldwin of Flanders, a prominent leader, was to reign as emperor in Constantinople and to rule over most of what is now Greece. Boniface was dissatisfied, however, and war broke out between Boniface and Baldwin. At this stage Doge Dandolo of Venice intervened and arranged a diplomatic solution satisfactory to all concerned. In return for the Doge's help, Boniface ceded to Venice the island

CRETE UNDER THE VENETIANS

of Crete, at a nominal price of 1,000 silver marks. On 12 August 1204 he signed the famous document of cession, the *Refutatio Cretae*, and this became the legal root of title by which Venice held the island.

The Venetians, being engaged at this time in securing their rights in Constantinople and in other parts of the Roman Empire, neglected to take possession of Crete. In 1206, Errico Pescatori, the Genoese pirate and self-styled Count of Malta, landed an army on the island and occupied Iraklion, the capital, where a Genoese fifth column had already been organised. He met no resistance in the countryside and consolidated his position by building fourteen or fifteen forts (*castelli*) in readiness for a Venetian invasion.

In the autumn the Venetians sent a fleet of thirty galleys with three admirals aboard. In methodical Venetian fashion, they did not sail straight to Crete, but paused first at Corfu where another Genoese pirate, one Leo Vetrano, had established himself. After recovering possession of both the citadel and the island of Corfu, the Venetians proceeded to Cretan waters. They met and defeated three or four of Pescatori's ships in the Gulf of Mirabello and then returned to Venice for the winter. In the spring of 1207 a larger squadron set out for Crete. On its way it encountered and defeated a Genoese force under Vetrano, who was captured and impaled. As they sailed southwards along the coast of the Peloponnese, the Venetians took the opportunity of occupying the forts of Coron and Modon which had been allocated to them on the division of the Roman Empire in 1204. The force at last reached Crete and after a violent struggle captured Iraklion and a large part of the island. Pescatori, who retained possession of many strongly defended posts, was reinforced from Genoa in 1208 and 1210, but it was clear that the Venetians would win in the end. Pescatori therefore negotiated terms and after a financial settlement withdrew his forces from Crete.

Thus, after a five-year struggle, the Venetians were at last masters of the island, and the first Duke of Crete, Jacob Tiepolo,

CRETE

took up his office. In taking full possession of their new colony the Venetians occupied and subsequently maintained most of Pescatori's forts. The names of some of these, and of other Venetian forts, have survived to the present day in such Cretan provinces as Selinon, Mirabello, Kainoúrgio (Castel Nuovo) and Monofátsi (Bonifacio).

COLONY OF VENICE

The first wave of colonists arrived on the island in 1211, to be followed by others in 1222, 1233 and 1252. Under the Venetians, the society of Crete had a strictly feudal structure. The colonists were drawn from the six districts (*sexteria*) of Venice, the men from each of which formed a separate division and were allocated to their own part of the island. The land in the immediate neighbourhood of Candia—as the Venetians called the capital city (now Iraklion)—was not given to individuals but remained the property of the state. This area corresponded roughly to the modern provinces of Malevísi and Témenos, with a small part of Pedhiadha. Ecclesiastical property was also exempted from general distribution and was reserved for disposal at the discretion of the Venetian government.

Within each of the *sexteria*, the lands were divided among the colonists under the local charge of a captain (*capitaneus*) who had the duty of installing the settlers in their fiefs. The colonists were either knights (*milites*, *cavalieri*) or commoners (*pedites*, *sergentes*), and each man was given a written agreement drawn up under oath setting out his rights and also his duties towards the Venetian Republic.

Each colonist was allocated a single fief, made up of one or more villages or smaller settlements and graded in size according to rank, a knight's fief being equal in size to six commoner's fiefs. To each commoner's fief was assigned a labour force of twenty-five villeins (*villani*, *parici*) to work the land. The villeins were the christianised descendants of the Arab colonists and were tied by the Venetians to the land, hence the frequent references to fugitive villeins being returned to their masters after an uprising. Each Venetian colonist also had a permanent residence in Iraklion and a right to grazing on the city lands.

Civil and military administration

Crete was governed from Iraklion, which remained the capital throughout the Venetian occupation until it fell to the Turks in 1669. The highest civil and military power was in the hands of the Duke, who was a Venetian nobleman elected by the Venetian Assembly for a period of two years. A palace was provided for him in the capital and he was paid a salary of 1,000 ducats a year. After the Duke came the two counsellors (*consiliarii*), who were elected in the same manner for two years. These three made up the ruling body of the island, called the *signoria*; their decisions were by majority, and the Duke was chairman *ex officio*. Governors (*rectores*) were also sent out from Venice, each with two counsellors, to the cities of Rettimo (Rethymnon) and Khania in western Crete.

In the country the original sub-divisions were replaced by *castella*, each commanded by a *castellan*, who exercised both civil and military powers in the district surrounding his garrisoned fortress. The *castellans*, about twenty in number, were either sent out from Venice or chosen by the Cretan *signoria* from Venetians in Crete. The *sexteria* themselves were replaced in the fourteenth century by four districts (*territoria*), each having as its capital one of the main cities of Crete: Khania, Rethymnon, Iraklion and Sitia. These regional sub-divisions of Crete survived as administrative units throughout the Venetian and Turkish occupations and are almost unchanged to the present day. The Venetian *Territoria* of Khania, Rethymnon and Iraklion have virtually the same boundaries and the same regional capitals as the present Nomoi of Khania, Rethymna and Iraklion: in the east of the island, the Venetian *Territorio* of Sitia has been extended westwards and renamed the Nomos of Lassithi, its present capital being the relatively new town of Ayios Nikolaos.

CRETE

Throughout the island, the Venetian fiscal services were under the charge of officials called chamberlains (*camerarii*), originally two in number, later four. The chamberlains had the power to act as substitute counsellors, but their main task was the collection of taxes, for which purpose they had a large staff of administrators, tax-gatherers and secretaries.

Until the middle of the fourteenth century the administrative élite shared the military command of the island with the six captains of the *sexteria*. At that time the office of *Capitan General* was instituted; this officer was appointed by the Venetian Assembly for two years, and was second only to the Duke in rank and precedence. In the event of the death or incapacity of the Duke, the *Capitan General* replaced him until a successor was appointed and arrived in Crete. His usual responsibilities, however, derived from his position as commander-in-chief of the armed forces, which consisted of a small standing army of mercenaries maintained by Venice in the walled cities and the *castelli* of Crete and of local troops raised in an emergency by the feudal tenants. The other duties of the *Capitan General* included the construction and maintenance of all fortifications and, in the Roman tradition, of roads and other public works.

The sea defence of the island and its protection from invaders and pirates was assured by the Venetian navy. A base for the fleet was established at Iraklion and later a second at Khania. Stone-vaulted ship-sheds of great strength, known as *arsenali*, capable of withstanding bombardment by any weapons of the time, were built on the quaysides. In winter the naval galleys were laid up in them and repaired, and in summer when the fleet was at sea they were used for the construction of new ships.

In Iraklion, remains of only four *arsenali* can be identified at the present day. The vaults of a group of three form part of the customs warehouse and, farther to the east, stands the arch of a fourth, which is the sole remnant of a group of six, built in 1584. At Khania, Cretans and tourists dine in waterfront restaurants adjoining the Venetian harbour; the rooms are long and narrow,

CRETE UNDER THE VENETIANS

open to the sea, and have heavy and low stone-vaulted ceilings. These are now the only visible remains of a row of nineteen *arsenali* built 300 years ago at the foot of the *castello*, in the heart of the Venetian city.

The *Capitan General* of the armed forces and all the high-ranking administrators were chosen in Venice from among the Venetian nobility. They were salaried officials, paid from public funds, and appointed on written contracts usually for short periods of office. The lower ranks of the civil service were recruited from the Venetians in Crete and sometimes from indigenous Cretans of noble family. Chosen thus were the judges, who sat in three courts, and the *Advocatores Communes* who had roles analogous to those of examining magistrates and public prosecutors. In addition there were the constables (*justitiarii*) with jurisdiction over the markets and commercial life, and the sheriffs, responsible for public order and security, who were called Lords of the Night (*Domini de Nocte*) and had armed men under their command.

To complete the picture of the colonial administration as a model of that of Venice, there was the Greater Council (*Consilium Majus*) made up of all the colonists of noble birth. This body met every December and elected from among its number the standing council which advised the *signoria*. On occasions of particular danger to the colony an extraordinary council, called the Council of the Feudal Lords (*Consilium Feudatorum*), would meet. In the last years of Venetian rule there was also a council of twelve noble Venetians and six noble Cretans which met to consider local grievances and had power to refer them direct to Venice; this was known as the Eighteen (*Disdotto*).

All officers and servants of the state were subject to the most rigorous bureaucratic supervision. The rights and duties of every man from the Duke and commander-in-chief to the humblest public employee were set down in writing in minute detail. In addition, frequent missions arrived from Venice with terms of reference requiring them to examine and report on almost every aspect of the administration and of commercial

CRETE

life in order to ensure that the interests of the Most Serene Republic were not being neglected. In the earliest times five noble Venetians—the 'Wise Men' (*Sapientes, Savii*)—came to Crete every year to inspect and regulate mercantile traffic and the sailings of ships, and to inform against or punish those who broke the regulations. In times of crisis special envoys called *proveditori* were sent to the island; they had wide, almost plenary, powers in both executive and judicial matters, and held office for eighteen months. From the sixteenth century onwards, when Turkish pressure on Crete was mounting, envoys with completely dictatorial powers were appointed, called *proveditori generali*.

The position of the Cretans

The Venetian power structure, imposed as though upon a political vacuum, made little acknowledgement of the existence of the Cretan ruling class. Old-established estates were confiscated, rights and customs were swept away, and the Cretan aristocracy, which had been both wealthy and accustomed to respect, found itself faced with the loss of its property and its privileges. Cretans of all ranks and classes shared an additional grievance against the Venetians, who not only robbed them of their land and freedom, but attacked their religion. The Venetians, for all their profession of religious tolerance, drove out the Greek Orthodox archbishop and bishops, and handed over their cathedrals to Latin prelates appointed by the Pope. The lower orders of the Orthodox clergy, the priests and the monks, were allowed to remain, but were subjected to financial pressure and to other forms of discrimination.

The outrages committed against their Church, the seizure of their lands and the loss of their freedom led to the rapid build-up among the Cretans of an intense hatred for their foreign overlords. The dispossessed local nobility, united with their people, became the natural leaders in the long and unrelenting struggle of the Cretans against their Venetian oppressors. Bloody revolt was succeeded by bloody revolt, and throughout more than

CRETE UNDER THE VENETIANS

three centuries of occupation the Venetians in Crete enjoyed only a few consecutive years of peace.

CRETE'S IMPORTANCE AS A COLONY

The location of Crete relative to Venice and her scattered eastern possessions gave the island a particular strategic value to the Venetians. Their main trade routes lay through the Adriatic and Aegean Seas to Cyprus and Egypt and to Constantinople and the Eastern Roman Empire. The passage of the Adriatic had been assured by the Crusaders' destruction of Zara in 1203 and by Venice's own grip on the Dalmatian coast. Voyages to Constantinople, Cyprus and Egypt were protected by the Venetian forts of Coron and Modon. The convoys for Egypt and for the Venetian enclave in Constantinople proceeded via Crete where they assembled and awaited stragglers both on the outward voyage and on their return to Venice. Without a strong naval base in Crete, Venice would have had great difficulty in protecting her long-distance shipping from the constant menace of piracy.

Crete was far from being a mere staging post, however. Ships of Venice were loaded there with wheat and barley from the Messara, oil from the sun-scorched olive groves, cheeses from the mountain dairies and wine from the vineyards of Malevisi. There was timber from the pine trees of Mount Idha to build Venetian warships, and casks of tar to caulk them.

The earliest Venetian colonists in Crete had concentrated their agricultural efforts on cereal production. The rigid control of prices, imposed and enforced for centuries by the Venetian state, led to an eventual decrease in the area under cereals. Associated with this decline, there was an increase in the cultivation of wine grapes and olives for oil. By 1575, the area under vines was so great that the *Proveditor General* Foscarini forbade the planting of vineyards on all land which had not been so used during the preceding ten years. Malmsey was exported in great quantities and was popular throughout

CRETE

continental Europe and in the British Isles. Timber was required in large amounts for cooperage, and its export was at times limited to Venice and her dependencies. Travellers to Crete mention the cultivation of sugar cane in lowland districts and in 1428 a colonist called Marino Zanono was granted the right to grow sugar cane for ten years in the Apokorona. Cotton seems to have been sent to Venice in significant quantities, along with that from Egypt. Raw silk was exported to Venice and other European cities.

The problem of keeping Crete

The value which the Venetians set on their Kingdom of Crete is proved by their determined efforts to retain possession of it. The great distance separating Venice from Crete was not the least of their difficulties. High-ranking administrators, decisions on difficult political issues, reinforcements of troops in emergencies, military and naval supplies all took about a month to reach the island. A despatch from Crete could not therefore receive an answer from the Republic in much less than two months. This time-lag inevitably gave an immediate, if relatively short-lived, advantage to any attempt to wrest Crete from Venetian hands, whether by an internal revolt or by invasion. Trouble-makers on the island could also choose a moment when the forces of Venice were split up or deployed elsewhere. During much of the time that Crete was occupied, the Venetian Empire was strung out in a long, broken chain of possessions stretching for over 2,000 kilometres (1,243 miles) from Venice southwards through the Adriatic and round the western coast of Greece to Crete, and then northwards through the Archipelago to Constantinople. Local troubles sometimes developed within the other colonies, either generated internally or provoked for political reasons by one of the enemies of the Republic; one such enemy was Genoa, with whom Venice was in continuous and bitter rivalry if not always openly at war. In the early years of Venetian occupation, the emperors of the Eastern Roman Empire, hoping to regain Crete and others of their

CRETE UNDER THE VENETIANS

former possessions, often encouraged the Cretans to revolt; later on, the Turks did the same. All the while, a continuous battle was fought against pirates, some of whom set up island bases in the Aegean, and on one occasion in Crete itself.

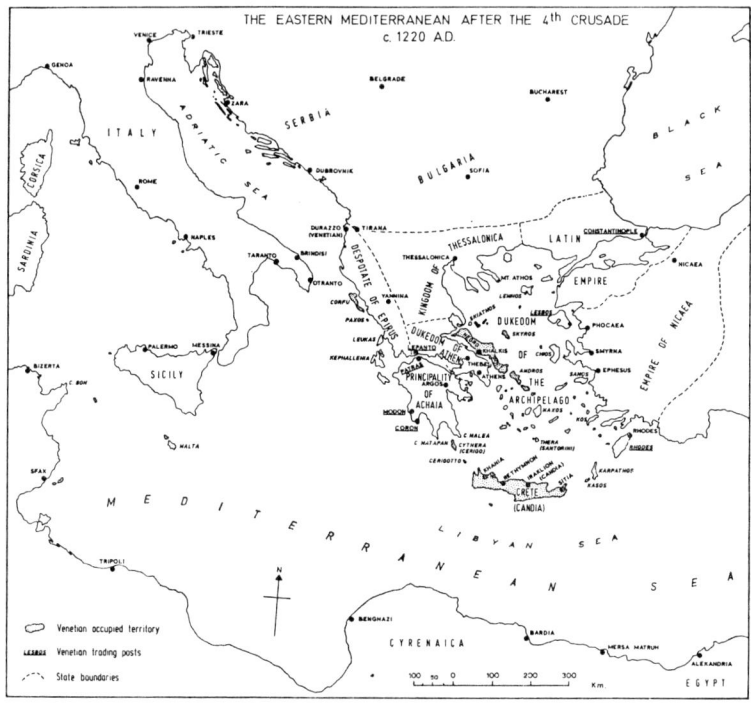

Most, if not all, of the Venetian colonists and many of the wealthier Cretan leaders occupied forts and other strongholds in their fiefs. These afforded valuable protection to both sides from pirates, local bandits and cattle raiders, besides their obvious use during the frequent bloody uprisings. Major local revolts, often lasting for several years and giving the Cretans temporary control over the greater part of the island, soon made the Venetians aware of any weaknesses which might exist in their system of fortifications. In 1230, a new fort was constructed

CRETE

on the small island of Soudha at the entrance to the long bay, and in 1282 a decade of disturbance was brought to an end in south-western Crete by the building and garrisoning of the large fort of Selino, now called Palaiokhora Selinou. Like many others, such as Ierapetra, Spinalonga, Grabousa and Rethymnon, the fort of Selinon was sited on a coastal promontory and served to show the Venetians' strength and preparedness against prospective seaborne invaders and the Cretans themselves.

The Venetians held Crete not only by virtue of their military strength and the brutality with which they put down revolts, but by making formal truces with individual members of certain leading Cretan families. From the time of the Treaty of the Two Syvríta in 1236, Cretan nobles were given privileges and security of land tenure equivalent to those of the noble Venetian colonists. At the end of several major revolts, the temporary loyalty of the rebel leaders was bought with grants of land and money. Thus many of the dominant Cretan families became not only the leaders of their people, but influential landed proprietors, wealthy even by Venetian standards.

Many of the less important Cretans, however, lost their lands as a penalty for rebellion, and were either executed or formally outlawed. Outlaws, dedicated rebels and victims of unsuccessful rebellions retreated in the traditional manner to the main mountain strongholds of Sphakia, Psiloritis and Lassithi and to other equally inaccessible parts of the island. Here they lived apart, becoming at times a serious threat to Venetian control over Crete by ambushing the routes to the south where they passed through the mountains.

THE CRETAN REVOLTS

The Venetian colonists had hardly settled into their new possessions in 1211 before the first revolt broke out against them. The Cretans recovered possession of a great part of eastern Crete and their success was such that the Duke was forced to call in outside aid. Further serious revolts took place in 1217-19

CRETE UNDER THE VENETIANS

and 1230–6, after which there were only minor disturbances until 1261 when a major revolt was stirred up by Michael Palaeologus, Emperor of the Eastern Roman Empire. This revolt in which the powerful family of the Kallergai played a minor role was ended by treaty in 1265. In spite of the official peace, the Hortatzis family took advantage of the Venetians' involvement in a war with Genoa to continue the fight. They initiated a major campaign in 1272 and were finally defeated in 1278 by the combined forces of the Venetian army and the colonists. The Venetians were aided in their struggle against the Hortatzai by the Cretan Alexios Kallergis and his followers. After the Hortatzai fled from Crete, the Kallergai became paramount among the Cretans in riches, power and prestige, and in their friendship with the Venetian leaders.

During the next few years, however, Alexios gradually reorientated his policy and word of his subversive activities reached Venice. In 1283, Duke Jacob Dandolo arrived in Crete with secret orders to arrest Alexios and send him to Venice. Forewarned, Alexios slipped out of Candia by night and was then outlawed by the *Signoria*. So began the longest of the uprisings, which lasted for sixteen years and brought the rule of the Venetians into the greatest danger.

For ten years Alexios waged a brilliantly conducted and ruthless guerilla war against the Venetians, until all Crete was in his hands, except the city of Iraklion itself and a few coastal forts. At this time, Venice was at war with her constant rival, Genoa. In 1293, after twice defeating the Venetian fleet and capturing their admirals, the victorious Genoese sailed at once to Crete and took Khania. Their admiral, Andrea Doria, then asked for the assistance of the Cretan rebels in driving out the Venetians, offering them the promise of freedom, but intending to annex Crete to Genoa. Most of the Cretan leaders were in favour of accepting the attractive proposals of the Genoese, but Alexios had greater foresight and realised that to do so would only bring Crete under the harsher rule of Genoa. It is recorded that he made a fighting speech to the Genoese envoys and ordered them to be gone. Dissension then arose in his own ranks and he lost the enthusiastic support of his followers. The Venetians were also at low strength, but managed to retake Khania from the Cretans and the few remaining Genoese. Everyone who could not escape by sea was put to the sword. There followed four years of guerilla warfare in the island until, in 1298, the last of the rebels were finally run to earth in Sphakia.

The Venetians, mollified by Alexios's outright rejection of the Genoese, and Alexios himself were willing to come to terms and negotiate a peace. After lengthy negotiations and the exercise of considerable diplomacy and perseverance, a treaty was agreed between them—appropriately entitled *Pax Alexii Callergii*. In addition to the restoration of his lands, Alexios was given extra fiefs and other important privileges. Both sides faithfully observed their obligations under the treaty, and Alexios remained a faithful friend of Venice throughout the rest of his lifetime.

Members of the Kallergis family continued to support the Venetians throughout the first half of the fourteenth century. When, in 1333, the Duke imposed an additional tax upon the Cretans, there were local rebellions in many country districts; 1,500 men marched on Iraklion and the whole country west of Almyros was in the hands of the rebels—only the castles held out. The Venetians sent a strong force from Venice and with the help of George Kallergis put down the revolt with some severity. The peace thus obtained lasted for only eight years before it was broken by Leon Kallergis, leader of that part of the family which had been unwilling to join in the general reconciliation with the Venetians. The ringleaders, with the exception of Leon Kallergis, were captured almost at once. Cornaro, then Duke of Crete, invited Leon and some of his relatives to Iraklion on the pretext of conferring honours upon them in return for their loyalty to Venice. While being formally and hospitably entertained to lunch by the Duke and other Venetian officials, Leon Kallergis was suddenly seized and bound. He was held without trial, interrogated under torture and condemned to death for treachery. He was executed by being sewn into a sack and thrown into the sea at night. The Duke, subsequently reprimanded by the Venetian government for having acted in secret, replied that he had done so to spare the feelings of the Kallergis family! The death of Leon enraged the insurgents still more, and they continued to harry the Venetians. In spite of assistance from Alexios Kallergis, grandson of the old Alexios, Venetian rule was not firmly re-established throughout the island until 1347.

The Venetian colonists' revolt

The severity with which the Most Serene Republic maintained control over her largest and most valuable colony not only alienated the Cretan population but at one stage caused the Venetian colonists themselves, with Cretan support, to rise up in revolt. The settlers depended for their living upon the production of cereal crops which they were not allowed to export but had to sell at artificially low, fixed prices on the island, either to the military commissariat or under strict control in the market place. Thus many colonists fell into arrears with their taxes and in paying their retainers. Added to this were the unauthorised levies imposed by *castellans* and other Venetian officers. The colonists were treated by the Republic as second-class citizens. They were not allowed to hold any of the profitable offices in the island such as Duke, counsellor, *castellan* or chamberlain, nor could they sit in the Greater Council at Venice, as they had had the right to do before they had emigrated. Matters came to a head in 1363, after the Duke had refused to allow the colonists to send a deputation to put their case to the assembly in Venice.

On 9 August, while the *Signoria* was meeting in the ducal palace, a crowd of armed settlers burst in by a back door and seized the Duke and the counsellors. They disarmed the guard at the palace and also the naval detachment at the port. They then immediately announced the end of Venetian rule and

CRETE

proclaimed an independent autonomous republic under the name and patronage of the Apostle Titus, the patron saint of Crete.

One of their first objectives was to win the support of the Cretans in the inevitable struggle against the Venetians. To this end they announced the equality of the Orthodox church with the Latin, and allowed Orthodox services to be held in the church of St Titus. Thus the Republic of St Titus presented a strong and united front while it awaited reaction from Venice. On hearing of the revolt, the Venetian Assembly, in a vain attempt to regain control by peaceful means, sent envoys to Crete with offers of free pardons, but the colonists expressed determination to defend their new Republic with the last drop of their blood. The Venetians had no alternative but to prepare for war.

In the winter months of 1363–4, Venetian agents throughout Italy and Germany recruited mercenaries numbering 1,000 cavalry and 2,000 infantry, while general mobilisation in Venice brought up to full strength the army and the fleet of thirty-three galleys and twelve transports. Five *proveditori*, chosen as representatives of the Assembly and given full powers in civil matters, were instructed to execute without trial ten named ringleaders of the rebellion, and to try the rest and sentence them to death, banishment or imprisonment as might seem appropriate. An agent of the colonists obtained a copy of the list of those proscribed; this was published in Crete, where Tito Venieri, the leader of the revolt, added to it the names of colonists known to be in favour of surrendering, thus securing their continued allegiance to his cause. The colonists, in somewhat of a panic by this time, sent to Genoa to seek aid; this was refused, since a Venetian envoy had forestalled them.

The Venetian commander, Lucino Dalvermi, aware of the poor state of the colonists' forces, decided to land near Iraklion and annihilate them at a single stroke. On 6 and 7 May 1364 the Venetian fleet sailed into the western end of the Bay of Iraklion, and while the landing was in progress about a hundred mercenaries made their way towards Almyros for the purpose of looting the water-mills. They were ambushed by the rebels and cut to pieces; the finding of their barbarously mutilated bodies greatly enraged the Venetians. The colonists' army, occupying the narrow passage between the cliffs at Almyros and the sea, was no smaller than the Venetian force, but greatly inferior in training and leadership. On 9 May 1364, Dalvermi's battle-hardened mercenaries received the shock of the rebel's attack without flinching and, in a strong counter-attack, broke the colonists' ranks and sent them in headlong flight to the city and the hills.

The next day, the mercenaries systematically looted the suburbs of Iraklion. The citizens meanwhile offered the keys of the city to Admiral Mikieli, commander of the Venetian fleet, requesting that their lives and property should be spared. Shortly afterwards, when Dalvermi entered Iraklion, he ordered the gate on the landward side to be walled up against the mercenaries to prevent them from looting the city. Even then it was only saved from destruction when Dalvermi's provosts killed two of the ringleaders. The flag of St Mark flew once more over Iraklion, and the *proveditori* set about the bloody work of revenge.

Other Cretan uprisings

As long as the Venetian army and the mercenaries remained in the island, all was quiet. However, no sooner had the fleet set sail than revolt broke out again, led by the three Kallergis brothers, John, George and Alexios, together with the proscribed Venetian nobles. After collecting sufficient followers to fortify some strong points for use as bases, the brothers declared war on the Venetians in August 1364 'fighting under the flag of the Byzantine Empire for the liberation of the island and its unity with the Empire'. *Énosis* was a powerful rallying cry and the whole of Crete west of the plain of Iraklion, apart from the Venetian forts, was soon under the control of the rebels. When this state of affairs became known in Venice, the Doge and

Council gave consent for raising an army of Turkish mercenaries and for buying horses in Turkey for the war against the insurgents. The Pope, through his mouthpiece the Latin Patriarch of Constantinople, proclaimed that the Cretan war was a Holy War and granted General Absolution to anyone who would serve in it for one year either in person or by proxy. He thus placed it on a level with the crusades, but at the same time somewhat illogically authorised the recruitment of infidel Turks to fight on the Venetian side.

The revolt reached a climax in 1365 when 2,500 Cretans occupied several villages near Iraklion. In a pitched battle, the rebels were defeated by Jacob Bragadino, the Venetian *Proveditor*, who strangled all his prisoners. The survivors fled to Lassithi, where they were joined by the villagers from the Pedhiadha and from Mirabello, Ierapetra and Sitia who brought with them all their livestock and movable possessions. Organised raiding from Lassithi supplied the rebels with provisions, and caused the Venetian commander, Peter Mocenigo, to retire to Iraklion. The *proveditori*, who had just mobilised 500 Turkish mercenary infantry and some cavalry, were forced to call for more aid from Venice.

In 1366 five new *proveditori* had some success against the rebels in all parts of Crete, and in the spring of 1367 collected such forces that the issue could no longer be doubted or delayed. The Venetians had 5,000 infantry and 400 cavalry, which they divided into two detachments. After a series of bloody engagements the two columns rejoined, having subdued central Crete, and took the war into Sphakia, the last stronghold of the Cretans. George and John Kallergis were taken prisoner by treachery in a cave where they had hidden, and Tito Venieri, the leader of the earlier revolt, was also captured. George was beheaded at Khania, and John and Venieri were executed at Iraklion. After three years of fighting, the revolt collapsed; it was the last serious rising by the Cretans and their final attempt to wrest freedom from the Venetians.

The revolts and conspiracies of the fifteenth and sixteenth

CRETE UNDER THE VENETIANS

centuries were small local affairs, easily put down by the Venetian authorities in the island. Not only had the Cretans become demoralised by the loss of much of their native aristocracy, but the agricultural and other resources on which they depended had been seriously reduced by the systematic destruction practised by both sides. The Venetians on their part were determined that there should never be another opportunity for the Cretans to rise against them.

THE GROWING TURKISH MENACE

Crete remained quiet for nearly a century after the rebellion of the Kallergis brothers, but Venice had to contend with more and more frequent piratical raids on the island by the Turks, especially after the fall of Constantinople in 1453. Fourteen villages in Sitia were destroyed in 1471 and in a similar Turkish attack in 1498 the monastery of Our Lady of the Headland at Toplou was pillaged. In the middle of the fifteenth century the fief-holders petitioned to have Iraklion fortified. The construction of the great walls and moat continued for about a hundred years. In 1485 an annual sum of 10,000 ducats was voted for the fortifications, of which one-quarter was contributed by the central Venetian government, and three-quarters by the fief-holders, townspeople, Jews, clergy and monks 'to defend them against this most truculent, most savage, most impious, yet most powerful enemy the Turk'.

Throughout the sixteenth century Turkish raids upon the towns and villages of Crete continued and increased in frequency. Often the Turks were aided by pirates of other nationalities, such as those from Algiers. In 1567, the Turks took Soudha in a night attack, sacking and burning the town. They then attacked Khania, which was saved by the Rector who, with 800 Corsican mercenaries, made a courageous sortie and drove the Turks back to their ships. At the same time the Algerian pirate, Ulutsalis, led a fleet of fifty galleys to the aid of the Turks, who were then at war with Venice. The forces landed at several places on the north coast of Crete and burnt some villages, putting the inhabitants to the sword. Finally Rethymnon, whose citizens had fled in terror, was sacked and burnt. The Venetians took this severe lesson to heart, and made several attempts to improve their seaward defences. Between 1572 and 1577 they built a strong new fort on the little island of Soudha in the entrance to the Bay, and new forts also at Grabousa in western Crete and on Spinalonga Island to the east.

By 1571 Venice had lost to Turkey all her possessions in Greece, and also Cyprus which, like Crete, she had called a Kingdom. Crete was defended for almost another century, until 1669.

During this period events within Crete occasionally led to local uprisings against the Venetians, thus adding to their problems. The unsuccessful Venetian defence of Cyprus in 1570-1, for example, led to considerable demands being made upon the Cretans for military service and for corvées. This led to a rising in the mountainous western provinces of Selinon, Sphakia, Riza and Kydonia which was suppressed with considerable brutality by the Dictator Cavalli. His ruthless methods aroused such horror among the other Venetians as to cause a change in the attitude of the ruling class in Venice towards the Cretans. Cavalli was succeeded by an enlightened and pro-Cretan *proveditor* who exercised clemency and moderation, and was thereby able to regain the allegiance and goodwill of the Sphakiots. The next *proveditor*, who took office in 1574, was Foscarini, probably the wisest and most enlightened Venetian administrator ever to be sent to Crete. He did much to halt the advanced disintegration of the feudal system by registering the fiefs and their owners, and by training a body of 1,200 knights he built up once more a formidable fighting force. Foscarini also made great efforts to improve the economic condition of Crete, which was by that time extremely poor.

The long and relentless oppression of the Cretan people by the Venetians led to a high emigration rate. In 1585, an official

CRETE UNDER THE VENETIANS

report by the Venetian Bailiff in Constantinople deplored the constant influx of Cretan refugees and noted the increase in their numbers caused by famine in the island. He reported that a significant number of the skilled craftsmen in the shipyards of the city were at that time Cretans. Worst of all, they were a danger to Venice by describing to the Turks the pitiful condition of the fortifications in Crete, the lack of food and of warlike supplies, and the weakness of the garrisons. They also told the Turks that the people of Crete desired a change of rulers and a relief from the present tyranny. The Turks were thus encouraged by reports of its weakness to focus their attention on Crete, the last Venetian stronghold in the eastern Mediterranean.

8 CRETE SINCE THE SEVENTEENTH CENTURY

ON 24 June 1645 Sultan Mahomet IV, without declaring war on Venice, landed a force of 50,000 men on the west coast of Crete. The fort of St Theodore near Khania was taken at once, and two months later Khania also fell. Rethymnon was overrun soon afterwards and by 1 May 1648 Iraklion itself was under siege. The city was to hold out alone for twenty-one years. Venetian attacks on the coasts of the Turkish empire provided diversions but gave the defenders of Iraklion no real respite. In 1660 Louis XIV of France sent some troops under the command of the Marquis de Ville, but they were too few to be of any use; an attempt to retake Khania was not successful. However, the French king's gesture impressed the Turks and the Grand Vizier Ahmed Köprulu came to Crete and took personal command of the besiegers. Francesco Morosini, already distinguished in the service of Venice and descended from a long line of soldiers and proconsuls, was governor of Iraklion and commander-in-chief of the fortress. The formal 'great siege' of Iraklion began in May 1667.

THE SIEGE OF IRAKLION

The first recorded significant sortie was made under the Frenchman de la Feuillade on 16 December 1667. It was repulsed with such losses that no further attempt to break out was made until reinforcements arrived in the following year. Early in 1668 Louis XIV recalled the Marquis de Ville on account of his inaction. The Venetian Senate at once invited another French officer, the Marquis de St André-Montbrun, to replace him, with the rank of Captain-General of the Land Armies of the Republic. St André-Montbrun was already well known to the Seigneurie of Venice for his personal bravery and for his success as a commander-in-chief in the Italian and German wars. He arrived in Iraklion and reported to Morosini on 21 June 1668. On the following day he reviewed the tiny garrison, a mere 4,500 men, who had the task of defending 3 kilometres of city walls. He then set about repairing and reorganising the shattered defences, while keeping the Turks at bay.

Almost a year later, on 19 June 1669, a French fleet with 6,000 soldiers on board arrived off Iraklion. With this support, the High Command at Iraklion planned attacks at several points round the coast of Crete in order to divert as much of the Turkish army as possible from the siege. The newly arrived commanders, the Duc de Navailles and the Duc de Beaufort, would have none of this audacious yet farsighted strategy. Without taking either Morosini (the commander-in-chief) or St André-Montbrun (the Captain-General) into their confidence, they planned an immediate sortie against the weaker of the two Turkish encampments, which was on the seashore facing the south-western bastion of Sabionéra. St André-Montbrun soon heard of the plan and, with Morosini, attempted to persuade the insubordinate dukes to postpone their proposed attack until further reinforcements arrived. If they would not wait so long, at least let them take with them some of the seasoned troops from the garrison. 'But they (Frenchman-like, mightily satisfied in themselves) would neither defer it nor have other than Greek guides with them'. The sortie, which took place on 25 June, less than a week after the troops landed, was a complete failure and was repulsed with many casualties.

Morosini and St André-Montbrun continued to press for offensive action in the form of diversionary attacks on the coast behind the Turkish lines, but nothing of the kind was attempted. The Grand Vizier was allowed to concentrate his whole strength

CRETE

before the walls of Iraklion. Another sortie, planned by de Navailles and de Beaufort, was made on 24 July and this, like their earlier effort, ended in disaster.

Then on 31 August 1669 the Duc de Navailles embarked his troops and ignominiously set sail for France, leaving Morosini, the Duc de Beaufort and the city to their fate. On 5 September Morosini capitulated on honourable terms.

Had the counsels of Morosini and St André-Montbrun prevailed, the Turks might well have been driven off and Crete saved for Venice. Certainly the Turks had learnt to respect the quality of the original defenders of the city, if not that of the fugitive French. In his despatch to the Prince de Condé, written two days later, St André-Montbrun commends the courtesy and civility of the Grand Vizier, whose behaviour, he says, 'ne sent rien le barbare'. Summing up the operations he says that the fall of the city may be attributed mainly to the small numbers of the defenders; counting French, Venetian and Greek, they amounted to only 7,000 or 8,000, confronting 30,000 Turkish troops, better turned out than any army in Europe. He also comments on the superior military engineering of the Turks. He concludes that Turkey, while set on continuing the war with Venice, does not wish to engage in a war with France.

The siege of Iraklion excited great interest at the time among students of military engineering and of siege works. Some of the Turkish works are described in detail in St André-Montbrun's despatches: he notes also that several of the German princes sent engineers to observe the siege and to take note of the construction of the Turkish works. The expert sent by the Elector Palatine was taken on a conducted tour of the city defences and at first professed himself unable to see the Turkish redoubts because, contrary to European practice, so little of them was visible above ground. The infantry tactics of the Turkish army were also studied and reported.

9 Mires: the bus station

10 *(left)* men relaxing [in]
a local café; *(below)*
schoolgirls walk throu[gh]
the streets of Mires,
showing interest in th[e]
stallholder's wares

CRETE SINCE THE SEVENTEENTH CENTURY

CRETE UNDER THE TURKS

Once Iraklion had fallen, the Cretans seem to have accepted the Turks as their rulers with comparative equanimity. There is no evidence of continued resistance by the Cretans to the Turkish conquest, although the men of Sphakia upheld their proud boast that they had never submitted to either Venetian or Turk. During the next 150 years large-scale disturbances only occurred in Crete when external events encouraged the Cretans to think that they could obtain outside assistance towards their goal of freedom. In the meantime, the actual status and living conditions of most of the native inhabitants of Crete were not greatly affected: they merely exchanged one alien master for another.

Religious persecution was mostly spasmodic in character and tended to be directed more against the higher echelons of the clergy than against the laity. In addition, all those who were not of the Moslem faith were subjected to various forms of economic discrimination; they were forbidden to hold land and were required to pay a heavy poll-tax. Many Cretans, skilled in the art of tax-evasion, derived satisfaction from a nominal conversion to Islam, in order to obtain the privileges of the faithful.

No serious rising against the Turks took place until 1692 when Domenigo Mocenigo, the Venetian Captain-General, gave naval support to a force of 2,000 Cretans who attacked Khania. The attack was not successful, and Mocenigo evacuated the whole of the Cretan force and settled them in the Peloponnese, which had been taken over for Venice by Francesco Morosini some six years before. The action of Domenigo Mocenigo in supporting the Cretans at Khania indicates that Venice had not abandoned all hope of recovering Crete. The island of Grabousa off the north-western tip of Crete had only been lost the year before, and both Soudha Island in the entrance of Soudha Bay and Spinalonga Island in the Gulf of Mirabello remained in Venetian possession until 1715.

CRETE

After Mocenigo's withdrawal Crete was quiet for some eighty years, the only disturbances being local ones caused by the excesses of Turkish officials. The Turkish government did nothing to develop or even to maintain the economic life of the island. They collected the poll-tax on every Christian and Jew, and made a levy of up to one-seventh on all agricultural produce, but the infrastructure on which high productivity depended was almost completely neglected. The roads were not systematically repaired and the harbours of Rethymnon and Iraklion were allowed to silt up.

In 1770 the Cretan leader Daskaloyanni obtained a promise of support from Russia, at a time when a Russian fleet under Admiral Elphinstone, ex-RN, was sailing round from the Baltic to engineer revolts against the Turks in Greece and other Mediterranean countries. Daskaloyanni had raised a force of 800 men, and for a time held the Turks at bay near Khania. The Russians arrived in the Aegean and defeated the Turkish fleet off Chios, but did nothing else to help the Cretan rebels who could not hope to hold out on their own. After the inevitable defeat of his followers, Daskaloyanni was executed with the usual Turkish barbarity. His name has been given to one of the principal squares of Iraklion. Henceforward for fifty years, until the freedom of Greece from Turkish rule was proclaimed at Ayia Lavra in 1821, Crete was quiet.

THE WAR OF GREEK INDEPENDENCE

In the early years of the nineteenth century, a great movement for independence grew up in Greece. It concentrated initially in the Ionian Islands and on the mainland but, idealistic and fierce though it was, the movement never really fully extended to Crete. Its success did, however, encourage two localised Cretan revolts.

The first of these took place in the summer of 1821 when the men of Sphakia rose up in arms to avenge the massacre of thirty Christians at Khania and the murder of the Metropolitan and

CRETE SINCE THE SEVENTEENTH CENTURY

five bishops at the cathedral altar in Iraklion. The Sphakiots laid siege to Khania by land, while ships from Kássos blockaded it by sea. The main Greek fleet, however, gave the Kassiot blockade no support, and little help was forthcoming from the revolutionary forces of the Greek mainland. By the spring of 1824, the rising was over—partly crushed by Egyptian troops summoned by the Sultan, Mahmud II, and partly hamstrung by the intransigent dissidence of the Sphakiots.

Crete was then quiescent until after the battle of Navarino (27 October 1827) in which the Turkish fleet was destroyed by an allied fleet of British, French and Russian ships. When news of this victory reached the island of Grabousa, the inhabitants seized the opportunity to raise the standard of freedom. For many years Grabousa had been a base for pirates, but now its rulers called themselves the Council of Crete, and sent one of their leaders, an Epirot called Hadjimichalis, into Crete to stir up revolt. He was defeated by the Turks at Frangokastello in 1828, captured and cut into small pieces. Subsequently, at the request of the first President of Greece, John Capo d'Istria, the British suppressed the self-styled Council of Crete on the pretence that it was a nest of pirates.

Despite the failure of this revolt, Crete, like other Greek lands still subject to the Turks, sent representatives to the Fourth National Assembly of Greece, held at Argos on 23 July 1829. However, when in 1832 Prince Otto of Bavaria became the first king of Greece, Crete was not included in his realm.

CRETE UNDER THE EGYPTIANS

Between 1822, when Egyptian troops were first summoned to Crete, and 1840, the island was governed on behalf of the Sultan by the Viceroy of Egypt. In 1830 Egyptian rule received the official sanction of the Powers—Great Britain, France, Italy and Russia—who had taken Crete nominally under their protection. The Egyptians were unpopular with both Moslems and Christians in Crete. More than 30,000 Christians left the island during this period, thinking that their cause had been finally abandoned by the Christian Powers. With the departure of many of the more turbulent elements of Cretan society, Osman Nur-ed-din Bey, the military commander, succeeded within a few months in taking control of the island without bloodshed. Law and order were established and the Governor-General, Mustafa Pasha, assured the Christians that 'the sole object of their Master, Mehemet Ali Pasha, was to establish tranquillity and to cause the prosperity of Crete, and to deliver the Christians from the vexations to which they were formerly exposed'. Two mixed judicial tribunals of Moslems and Christians were established, one at Iraklion and the other at Khania. Many former injustices were discontinued and this, together with an improvement in trading prospects, encouraged the return of many of the voluntary exiles and attracted other Greeks by offering the prospects of profitable business in the towns. Villages were re-peopled and agriculture began to revive.

However, as soon as Mehemet Ali perceived that his new dominion was prospering and that it had great latent potential, his greed was aroused. He cowed the new tribunals by executing a Moslem member and banishing two others to Grabousa. Then, already with the right to one-seventh of the revenue of Crete, he introduced a tax on all wine produced, whether drunk at home by the producer or sold, increased the export duties on olive oil, and taxed many other commodities for the first time.

By the autumn of 1831 Crete was once more under the rapacious and tyrannical rule of an absent Moslem prince. But worse was to come in 1833 when Mehemet Ali briefly visited Crete in person. He invited the Cretans to submit a memorandum setting out their grievances and in due course a petition was submitted via the Pasha. This enumerated some of the many unpopular taxes, complained of the excesses of the troops in the villages, and requested less severity in the application of the *bastinado*, a punishment consisting of beating with thin sticks on the soles of the feet and on the abdomen. Mustafa Pasha dared not present such a document to his master and instructed his secretary to draw up a memorandum expressive 'only of happiness and affection'. It was signed by forty or fifty Greeks in the pay of Mustafa Pasha and appears to have deceived Colonel Campbell, the British Consul-General, who accompanied Mehemet Ali.

The nadir was reached when Mehemet Ali forced the tribunal of Khania to publish a proclamation which included detailed and harsh instructions concerning the redistribution of the population, redeployment of agricultural labour, cultivation of the land, collection of additional taxes, and official appropriation of large areas.

The fear and consternation caused by the proclamation spread to the whole of the island and a traditional Cretan Assembly of elders, mainly Moslems, met at Mourniés, 5 kilometres from Khania. This Assembly sent deputations to the four Allied Powers thinking that they would protect them from the oppressive new decree. The members of the Assembly, some thousands in number, took up their residence under the trees around Mournies, resolving to remain in permanent session until answers were received. A proclamation of 22 September 1833, which promised redress of almost all their complaints, was accepted by many of those present at the Assembly, with the result that only a hard core of doubters remained. By 8 November, almost exactly three months after Mehemet Ali had arrived in Crete, the Assembly had dwindled to less than a hundred.

Meanwhile Osman Nur-ed-din, now a Pasha, had arrived in Soudha Bay with a squadron of Egyptian warships. He went at once with Mustafa Pasha to Mournies, taking an escort of some 250 infantry and 60 cavalry. They arrested six of the unarmed peasants, but released them almost at once. Two days later an Egyptian corvette landed 200 men and brought the news that 4,000 more were on their way. The corvette seems to have brought new orders to the Pashas in Crete, since on 11 November they went to Mournies and arrested without resistance

CRETE

thirty-three of the peasants who were still there. The Pashas proclaimed that the obstinate men whom they had arrested would be thrown into chains. Mehemet Ali, however, demanded that blood should flow and, in spite of the protests of the Pashas themselves and those of the French Consul at Khania, ten of the thirty-three imprisoned peasants were taken back to Mournies and hanged. The night before, twenty-one people had been arrested and executed in different parts of the island.

DIRECT TURKISH RULE

The Convention of London, 15 July 1840, required of Mehemet Ali that he should evacuate Crete, Syria and Arabia; in return he received the hereditary powers of Khedive of Egypt. In 1841 the Sphakiots rose in arms and formed a provisional government with a view to union with Greece. This rebellion was crushed by the Turks, and the Greek King Otto was blamed for not having sent help. The idea of uniting Crete with Greece was widely supported at this time; a 'Central Committee of the Cretans' was formed on the Greek mainland and Lord Palmerston supported the proposal in England. In the spring of 1853 Tsar Nicholas I of Russia, who wished to remain in agreement with England on the Eastern question, suggested that the British should take over both Crete and Egypt in return for a general Russian protectorate over the Orthodox subjects of the Turkish Empire. The reaction of the British ministers and their ultimate rejection of these proposals led directly to the Crimean War in March 1854.

The Treaty of Paris, 30 March 1856, which ended that war and guaranteed 'the independence and the territorial integrity of the Ottoman Empire', also contained an express repudiation of any right to interfere in the internal affairs of Turkey. So far as the peoples under Turkish rule were concerned, this meant that the Sultan could treat them as he chose; if he wished to persecute them there was no one to whom they could appeal. Theoretically this freedom from outside interference imposed a duty on the Sultan to act reasonably, but, by 1860, reports were reaching Britain of 'almost inconceivable misgovernment obscurantism and tyranny' throughout the Ottoman Empire.

Crete was not exempted from the general oppression. In May 1866 a National Committee of Cretan chiefs met at Omalos, and a party of Turkish troops who came to arrest them was greeted with small-arms fire. In September a General Assembly of Crete, meeting at Khora Sphakion, proclaimed *énosis*—union with Greece. Turkey at once blockaded the island. The Cretans divided 'Free Crete' into three operational commands: western, central and eastern. The troops of the western command were defeated by Mustafa Pasha at Vaphés. The central command, under Koronáios, had established its headquarters south-east of Rethymnon in the monastery of Arkadhi which, in addition to its defenders, was crowded with refugees. Mustafa Pasha brought his artillery into position on the foothills of Idha which commanded the Cretan stronghold. In spite of fierce attacks by the Turkish troops who outnumbered them many times, the Cretans held out for two desperate and bloody days. Then the Turks forced their way in at the main gate. At this moment, when the courtyard and all the lower rooms were filled with men and women fighting for their lives, the chief of the monks, Igumenos Gabriel, set fire to the powder magazine. Almost 1,000 Cretans and twice as many Turks perished in the explosion, and their scattered bones were for some years a visible memorial of their fate. Gabriel himself was blown up with the monastery which he could no longer defend. The hopeless defence of Arkadhi and the heroic valour of the men and women who fought and died there is remembered by all Cretans with pride and gratitude and is commemorated at an annual festival on 10 November.

Meanwhile the friends of Crete had organised help from outside. The best known of the blockade-runners bringing in arms and food was the SS *Arkadhi* in which the Englishman J. E. Hilary Skinner travelled to Crete from Syria in March 1867. Built for blockade-running in the American Civil War, the ship was bought for service against the Turks by a subscription raised among expatriate Greeks, mostly in England. She is described as having 'a long grey hull with high paddle-boxes, and raking masts' and her British engineers were 'of pliant oily fingers, of large wages and plentiful bottled porter'. She penetrated the blockade more than twenty times before a Turkish warship drove her ashore near Cape Krio at the south-western extremity of Crete.

Skinner reached the north coast of Crete without incident and on his journey southwards saw the ruins of the monastery at Arkadhi, where the bodies of the dead still lay rotting. At Khora Sphakion he met some Americans with a small boat, which Skinner calls 'a neatly painted dinghy', and one torpedo. The plan was for their Greek pilot to swim off from the boat under cover of darkness one calm night and attach his torpedo to the hull of any Turkish ship which offered itself as a target. When he had swum away to a safe distance his companions in the boat would explode the charge electrically through a wire. After their first attempt failed, the second target chosen was a Turkish frigate anchored under the cliffs to the west of Khora Sphakion. The sentry on the frigate saw the Americans' boat and raised the alarm. The frigate slipped her cable, leaving an anchor buoy to mark the spot, and ran out a short distance from land. The Americans fixed a torpedo to her cable and when the Turks duly returned to weigh their anchor, the bomb was hauled up close to the bow of the frigate. All seemed set for success when it was found that the electric wire for detonating the charge was broken, and the Turks were able to haul the torpedo inboard and examine it at leisure. This is probably the first example of the attempted use of an electrically detonated explosive charge in European naval warfare.

The revolt, which had begun in 1866 and lasted until 1868, was only suppressed with the aid of Egyptian troops. In order to avoid future revolts and pacify the island once and for all, the Sultan promulgated a series of reforms embodied in what is known as the Organic Statute. This satisfied neither the Cretans

CRETE SINCE THE SEVENTEENTH CENTURY

nor the ruling class of Turks in Crete, and in 1876 the islanders presented fresh demands. The following year, when the outbreak of the Russo-Turkish War caused a ferment in the Greek provinces which were still subject to Turkey, a committee was formed to agitate for the independence of Crete. When its demands were refused by the Turks, an appeal was made to Great Britain to take Crete under a protectorate. This was refused, but the British Consul at Khania, Mr Sandwith, used his good offices to secure a large number of important changes in the Statute. These were embodied in the Pact of Halépa, so named from the suburb of Khania where the negotiations and signature took place. The Pact of Halepa, signed in 1878 in the house of the Mitsotakis family who had played a significant part in the negotiations, is today regarded by Cretans as the first decisive step on the road to freedom and to unity with Greece.

The Cretans were satisfied, but in such turbulent times satisfaction could not be permanent. In 1885, the time seemed ripe for Greece to take by force from Turkey the rest of the provinces of Thessaly and Epirus, parts of which had been ceded to her in 1881 at the insistence of the British. Greek forces were on several occasions in action against the Turks on the northern frontier, whereupon the European Powers called upon Greece to disarm. This she refused to do and the Powers, with the exception of France, set up a naval blockade. The Christians in Crete, who had been in control since 1878, proclaimed their union with the kingdom of Greece, but the blockade robbed their gesture of any meaning. In 1889 the Turks put pressure on Greece to persuade the Cretans to allow Turkish garrisons to occupy some fortresses in Crete. No sooner had the garrisons arrived when the Sultan annulled the Pact of Halepa.

After five years of seething discontent, the Cretans were given a Christian governor in 1894, but he was superseded in the following year by a Moslem. In the early months of 1896 civil war erupted in Khania between the Christians and the Moslems. The Sultan, under pressure from the European Powers, agreed to call a National Assembly of Cretans, to renew the Pact of

CRETE

Halepa, appoint a Christian governor and proclaim a general amnesty. On 4 September the new Governor, George Berovic, a former Prince of Samos, took office, but his authority lasted little more than five months, and war between the Christians and Moslems again broke out at Khania in February 1897. The Christians once again proclaimed union with Greece and this time received prompt aid. On 10 February Prince George, the second son of King George I of Greece, led a flotilla of torpedo-boats to intercept Turkish reinforcements, and on 15 February a Greek army commanded by Colonel Vassos landed west of Khania.

The admirals of the European Powers (Great Britain, France, Italy, Russia, Germany and Austria-Hungary), whose flag-ships were in Soudha Bay, sent an international landing party and put an end to the fighting by separating the combatants. They then occupied Khania and by that act ended for ever all but the shadow of Turkish rule in Crete.

Soon afterwards Germany and Austria-Hungary withdrew their ships from the international force at Soudha, leaving those of Great Britain, France, Italy and Russia. Khania was held by a four-power force, the British held Iraklion, the Russians Rethymnon, the French Sitia and the fort of Spinalonga, and the Italians Ierapetra. The governorship of Crete was offered in turn to a Swiss Federal Councillor, a Luxembourg colonel and a Montenegrin minister, all of whom refused to take it. The Cretans governed themselves as best they could through an Assembly which met at various places under the presidency of Sphakianakis. The Christians held all the open country while the Moslems were concentrated in the towns, most of them being in Khania. On 6 September 1898 an attack was made by some Turks on the British in Iraklion harbour, and the British vice-consul was murdered. In retaliation, the British naval commander bombarded the city. 'Admiral Noel's energy achieved what diplomacy had long striven to obtain; the ringleaders were hanged, and two months after the affray at Candia the last detachment of Turkish troops left the island; the fort on the islet in Soudha bay alone was henceforth occupied by Ottoman soldiers.'

Prince George of Greece was offered by the four protecting Powers the post of their High Commissioner in Crete. He was to hold office for three years under the suzerainty of the Sultan, and each of the Powers was to advance £40,000 towards the expenses of setting up the administration. Prince George accepted the office and landed at Soudha on 21 December 1898. The international naval forces withdrew at once, but the troops remained to police the island. In 1899 the first Assembly of Autonomous Crete, composed of 138 Christians and 50 Moslems met to consider the draft of a constitution which had been drawn up by a mixed commission presided over by Sphakianakis. The constitution in its final form permitted the Prince to appoint five 'councillors', of whom one had to be a Moslem, and to nominate ten members to the Chamber of Deputies. This was to meet every year and to have the rest of its members elected every two years. Sphakianakis, who had piloted the constitution through the Assembly, then retired from political life. The real architect of the constitution was a young lawyer called Eleftherios Venizelos, who in a long and distinguished career became indisputably the greatest of Greek statesmen.

In August 1904 Prince George was formally requested to 'inform the Great Powers of the firm resolution of Crete, and to urge them not to postpone its union with Greece'. In March 1905, seeing that nothing was being done or was likely to be done to assist their union with Greece, the Cretan leaders withdrew from the Chamber of Deputies and from the Assembly and united under Eleftherios Venizelos. They armed themselves and set up their headquarters in a house high in the White Mountains, above the village of Thérissos, from which they proclaimed the freedom of Crete and its union with Greece. Today a motor road leads from Therissos to 'Venizelos' House' which has become a place of pilgrimage for Cretan patriots. Venizelos and his Provisional National Assembly held out in the mountains until the winter, when they surrendered to the consuls of the four Powers. Prince George resigned and Alexander Zaimis, a former Prime Minister of Greece, became the new High Commissioner in September 1906. Crete remained quiet under Zaimis and became steadily more Hellenised. In July 1908 the Powers began to withdraw their troops.

In October 1908, the news that Bulgaria had proclaimed independence and that Austria had annexed Bosnia and the Herzegovina roused the Cretans once more. They demanded to be united with Greece, and the Powers accorded them *de facto* recognition, although they would not formally admit their claim. If the Greek politicians in Athens had had the courage to act in support of the Cretans it is likely that Crete would then have realised her secular dream. As it was, the Greek flag flew over Crete for only a month before the Powers returned and cut it down. The Greek army and navy mutinied in protest against their government's inaction and King George nearly lost his throne. Greece was thoroughly disorganised and badly led, and was only saved by Venizelos, who formed a new government in October 1910.

On 14 October 1912 Venizelos admitted Cretan deputies to the Greek Chamber, and declared that henceforth it would be the sole legislative assembly of both Greece and Crete. His announcement virtually coincided with Turkey's declaration of war on its former possessions of Serbia and Bulgaria, and Greece forestalled similar action against herself by formally declaring war against Turkey on 18 October 1912. The Greeks, Serbs and Bulgarians rapidly obtained sweeping victories over the Turks, and the war ended temporarily with the Treaty of London. Article 4 of the Treaty provided that Crete was to be ceded by the Sultan to the Balkan allies, but did not specifically name Greece. After further hostilities in which Crete was not concerned, the war ended with the Treaty of Bucharest which, among other things, dismissed a Bulgarian claim to Crete.

Greece and Turkey signed a treaty on 14 November 1913 in which a common frontier was delineated and Crete definitely

CRETE SINCE THE SEVENTEENTH CENTURY

assigned to Greece. The island was formally taken over on 14 December 1913 by King Constantine, at whose side were the Crown Prince George, who never became king, and Eleftherios Venizelos, the Prime Minister.

CRETE AS PART OF GREECE

From 1914 to 1940

In World War I Greece under King Constantine, although technically neutral, was at first obstructive to the Allied cause. Venizelos, who was supported by most of 'New' Greece—that part in fact which he had liberated from the Turk and the Bulgar—went first to Crete, and then via Lesbos to Thessaloniki, where he formed a provisional government which declared war on Bulgaria and Germany. Although Crete was outside the main stream of events, Soudha Bay was used as a base by the British and Allied fleets.

In the exchange of populations between Greece and Turkey following the defeat of Greece in 1920 by the Turks, Crete received her share of 'New' Greeks. They were settled in villages and suburbs of their own, many of which have names recalling the origins of their inhabitants. Iraklion, for example, has the suburbs of Néa Alikarnassós to the east and Néai Klazómenai to the south. Many whose families came from Turkey are still proud of their origin and show a strong belief in the superiority of their Asia Minor culture over that of Crete. Nevertheless they have settled down well and have made a great contribution to the development of Cretan agriculture and commerce.

Crete emerges only briefly from the 'confused chronicle of prejudice and self-interest in Greek political life between the wars'. In March 1935 an attempt was made by the Liberals under the Cretan Venizelos to overthrow the republican government and restore the monarchy. The army was disorganised, except in Macedonia, but the navy, manned largely by reservists, sailed from its base at Salamis. The rebel fleet, consisting of most of the serviceable units of the Greek navy and

CRETE

led by the battleship *Avéroff* with Venizelos on board, set course for Soudha Bay in Crete. It was pursued at first only by cries of derision from the Athenian press which called the *Averoff* a floating *taverna*. A more serious pursuit was mounted by a squadron of Hawker Harts of the Hellenic Air Force which scored a direct hit on the *Averoff* with a bomb, causing some damage to one of the forward deck guns. Venizelos was prepared for prolonged resistance in Crete, and had arranged for an oil tanker belonging to a member of his family to be on hand to refuel the fleet. However, all resistance on the mainland collapsed and Venizelos fled, with the officers of the fleet, to Rhodes, then in Italian hands. This was his last appearance on the political scene.

World War II

Life went on steadily and uneventfully in Crete until Greece was drawn into the war against Italy and Germany. On 28 October 1940 the Greek Government rejected an ultimatum by the Italians whose army already confronted them from the Albanian frontier. This was the Ὄχι (NO!) which resounds through Greek history, and is commemorated each year by a public holiday. The next day the first British troops landed in Crete, six days before the first British landing on the mainland on 3 November. On 14 November the Greek army began the counter-attack which threw the Italians out of Greece back into Albania. There they remained until 9 March 1941, when they mounted a new offensive which was so mauled by the Greeks that on 3 April Germany was forced to intervene by attacking Greece through Yugoslavia.

It became clear that Greece could not be held, and the Greek army capitulated to the Germans at Thessaloniki on 23 April. By 2 May the withdrawal to Crete of the British, Australian and New Zealand forces had been completed, and by this time also the Greek Government, led by the king, was established in Crete.

On 20 May 1941 the airborne invasion of Crete by the

CRETE SINCE THE SEVENTEENTH CENTURY

Germans began. Intelligence reports had been disbelieved, and the Germans achieved complete surprise. During the first day some 7,000 parachutists and glider troops landed on and around Maleme airfield west of Khania. The next day, several hundred troop-carrying gliders landed at various points on the north coast, until some 20,000 men had arrived with all their equipment. By contrast, seaborne attacks by the Germans on the nights of 21 and 22 May were repulsed—with the loss of two British cruisers and four destroyers. Soudha Bay was by this time untenable on account of enemy air attacks, and the few British tanks available had failed to dislodge the Germans from Rethymnon.

On 28 May the Italians landed unopposed at Sitia, and the Allied troops began to withdraw from the coast of Sphakia. The withdrawal continued until the night of 31 May; 14,580 troops escaped. The Allies lost 13,000 killed or captured in Crete, against German losses of 12,000–15,000. An area in the east of the island roughly corresponding with the Nomos of Lassithi was occupied by the Italians and the rest by the Germans. After the withdrawal of the regular units and of the Greek Government, a guerilla campaign was waged against the forces of occupation throughout Crete by Greek irregular bands staffed by British and Canadian officers and supplied by air and submarine from Egypt. British troops landed at Patras on 4 October 1944, but the German and Italian garrisons in Crete, 22,000 in number, did not surrender until 9 May 1945, the Cretan guerillas maintaining pressure on them until the end.

Postwar recovery and growth

The end of World War II left Crete with her cities and villages badly scarred and her economy in ruins. Exports had been virtually at a standstill, and the recovery of farming was retarded initially by the absence of able-bodied farmers. Even with the inbuilt strength of a peasant economy based on subsistence farming, the Cretans, especially in the towns, suffered severely in 1945. Civil war in mainland Greece meant that no aid was forthcoming from Athens, but a unit of the United Nations Relief and Rehabilitation Administration was standing by in Egypt and landed in Crete as soon as the German command had surrendered. Not long afterwards the New Zealand Government sent a large flock of pedigree sheep as a gift to the Cretans. This farsighted gesture did much to improve the local breed and enabled milk and cheese production, as well as the supply of meat, to increase more rapidly.

General progress in recovery and development was slow and in 1948 the Greek Government invited the International Health Division of the Rockefeller Foundation to make a survey of Crete with a view to improving its rate of development. The investigations, which took four years, covered every aspect of life and work in the island. Recommendations were made in the fields of agriculture, industry, transport, investment, tourism and public health, and the results were published in 1953. The foreword to the report concluded with the words: 'In view of the number of United Nations and United States agencies that have been working in Crete and Greece, the Rockefeller Foundation has not considered it necessary to implement the recommendations contained in this report.' Nor in fact did anyone 'implement' any of the proposals either then or during the next decade.

The step which set the island firmly on the path of development was not taken for another eleven years. Then, in January 1964, the Organisation for Economic Co-operation and Development and an Israeli commercial concern called AGRIDEV Ltd signed an agreement by the terms of which the company was to assist the Greek Government in drawing up an Economic Development Plan for Crete. The Israelis worked fast, and the plan was in the hands of the OECD by April 1965, but even its authors were afraid that it might 'remain a merely academic episode'. It was, however, approved by the Greek Government, and the Ministry of Co-ordination was ordered to put it into effect. The Regional Development Authority for Crete, the local office of the Ministry, took the matter in hand but was

11 A vineyard in central Crete: *(above)* sultanas drying in the sun; *(below)* the dried sultana grapes being packed for transport

12 Panormos: (*left*) a cooper at work; (*right*) the wine barrels lined up in the local vineyard

hampered by the fact that it could not exercise control over any of the executive ministries. Each of these had its own chain of command reaching back to Athens and was not receptive of suggestions from the Development Authority.

In 1970, a major reorganisation of the Civil Service took place in which the powers of the Ministry of Co-ordination were greatly increased and a special Minister for Crete appointed. The Development Plan has achieved its most spectacular successes in roadmaking, electricity supply, the expansion of irrigated agriculture and the reconstruction and extension of the harbour and airport of Iraklion. The increase in tourist traffic has far exceeded the expectations of the planners, and even the large number of new hotels and other units of tourist accommodation has barely succeeded in coping with the new peaks of demand.

The Litton episode

The large industrial corporations of the world had not interested themselves in Crete because it could offer no large-scale outlet for their products or services, but Litton Industries Inc, one of the largest American conglomerate corporations, had a different approach. The Corporation had in 1965 three main interests in the United States: business machines and computers, accounting for approximately 30 per cent of their sales; defence and aerospace material, including nuclear propulsion for ships (25 per cent); heavy industry, ship construction and electronics (45 per cent). These seemingly diverse and unconnected interests had one common link; this was the use of systems analysis, adopted from engineering and applied to management procedures in the form of organisation and method study and critical path analysis. Litton decided that they could apply this approach to national economic and industrial planning; in their own words they 'moved into the development business'.

In 1965 they opened discussions with the Greek Government for the negotiation of a contract. Litton offered to take over from the Greek State all responsibility for economic development in two regions, the north-west Peloponnese and Crete. Negotiations dragged on for two years against the kaleidoscopic backdrop of Greek internal politics. No result was achieved and the talks were on the verge of collapse when the military *coup d'état* of 21 April 1967 brought a sudden and dramatic change. In less than a month, on 15 May, the contract between the Greek Government and Litton was signed.

In simple business terms, the provisions of the contract were not favourable to Greece. Litton agreed to use its 'best efforts' to improve the standard of living in the two regions by securing foreign investment in projects within them. In return, Litton was to be repaid its expenses and 11 per cent, together with a commission of 1·9–2·25 per cent on the value of all foreign long-term loans and capital attracted. Payment, based on estimates, was to be made six months in advance in hard currency in Zurich. A development period of twelve years was envisaged with an initial contract from 1967 to 1970. During this time Litton undertook to secure $150 million of foreign investment, to be matched by $90 million of Greek domestic investment. Litton and its subsidiaries were not required to invest in the areas unless they chose to do so.

The operation began with a fanfare of publicity both in Athens and in Crete, but soon lost its initial impetus. Relations with the government became strained, and in addition internal conflicts developed within the Litton organisation. These resulted in the rapid turn-over of personnel in the higher echelons of management, which gave rise to lack of continuity. Problems of communications and cooperation with Greek and other officials further reduced working efficiency. In the Messara Plain, for example, a conflict of personalities between Litton's staff and an FAO team led to a total withdrawal by Litton from the area, although it had the highest agricultural development potential in Crete. This came shortly after an announcement by one of Litton's vice-presidents that 'we are using the Greeks as guinea-pigs' which received widespread and hostile publicity in the Greek press. By the beginning of 1969 it was obvious to all that the operation could not succeed. The Greeks had lost interest and Litton's organisation was in disarray. By March 1969 Litton had achieved one-sixth of its initial investment target in two-thirds of the contract period. In May, Litton reviewed the contract and began to look for loopholes, suggesting that the figures in the contract had been estimates and were not binding. Research and planning, in the case of Crete largely based on earlier work by others, continued with little attempt at implementation. In the autumn Litton announced that it would not seek renewal of its contract, and by the end of 1969 it had withdrawn from Greece. The offices in Athens and Crete were closed and a large quantity of paper was taken over by the Greek Government. The ministries concerned with carrying out the various parts of the Development Plan of 1965 carried on quietly with their work in spite of setbacks. In so far as the development of Crete was concerned, the Litton affair did little or no harm.

Monastery of Arkadhi, exterior

9   RURAL LIFE, TRADITIONAL AND MODERN

THROUGHOUT the long centuries of resistance against foreign rulers many Cretans—like Captain Micháles in Kazantzakis's novel *Freedom and Death*—were driven to fight by their passionate belief in a free Crete. The majority, however, were fighting not for an ideal but out of necessity to safeguard their families, their homes, their villages and their land. In earlier centuries, many Cretans were protected by the relative isolation of their mountain villages. Later, again partly because of their remoteness, some of these villages became famous centres of rebellion and were often the target of severe reprisals by the occupying power. Anoyia, for example, has been twice destroyed in the last 150 years—once by fire in 1822, by order of Sherif Pasha, and again on 15 August 1944 when the Germans systematically destroyed the entire village. The case of Anoyia, although dramatic, is not exceptional; numerous villages have suffered both from reprisals and from conventional war damage. A survey conducted after World War II estimated that in 225 Cretan villages, almost a quarter of the buildings were 50 per cent destroyed or more.

The long succession of rebellions and invasions has taken its toll of the rural buildings. Thus many villages, in spite of their early Greek names and very old sites, contain relatively few datable buildings of the medieval period or earlier. In spite of this, the ancient character of many villages is still preserved in their strongly nucleated appearance with the individual houses tightly clustered together on a hilltop, ridge or other defensible position. Seen at close quarters, they frequently retain the internal chaos of old, complex property boundaries and impenetrable streets designed for the donkey and the pedestrian rather than the motor car.

The dazzling white of the lime-washed outer walls contrasts sharply with the cool, gently lit interiors of the houses. The house of a village family is primarily a night-time fastness, a winter refuge and a store place. Its furnishings may be basic and simple, sometimes formal, but are rarely elaborate or self-conscious. Small ikons and religious pictures bear witness to the Christian devotion of the occupants; while transistor radios, portable gas stoves, tablecloths and household containers of brightly coloured plastics are evidence of their contact with the urban markets. Until relatively recently most cooking was done on outdoor charcoal grills, in the lime-washed domes of outdoor wood-burning ovens or, for a small fee, by the nearest baker. It is still a common sight in the larger villages and towns to see a woman or small boy hurrying down the street carefully carrying the midday meal in a shallow metal pan. Since World War II, however, the majority of rural families have invested in single or twin gas burners, fed by bottled gas—a revolution in domestic economy which has saved the last remnants of Cretan woodland from destruction.

Perhaps the most important changes in rural life since the war have been those resulting from the supply of electricity to the villages: lighting, refrigerators, cookers, radios, small motors, irrigation pumps and other domestic and agricultural equipment. In 1948 only 2 per cent of the rural communities had electricity, but the programme of rural electrification carried out in the 1960s brought a supply to almost every village and hamlet.

Other basic facilities are as yet fairly limited in most villages. In 1961, over 80 per cent of the rural households had no piped water supply, but obtained their water either from a public tap in the street (46 per cent) or from a nearby well or spring (38 per cent). There is usually a general store and, depending on the size of the village, several cafés and possibly a bakery, a barber's shop, and a petrol station. With increasing personal mobility, many of these facilities are becoming concentrated in the larger villages, which act as local service centres, and in the towns.

According to the 1971 Census, there are 1,317 villages in Crete, providing homes for 68 per cent of the island's population. Most of the villages are very small, having an average of about 200 inhabitants. Table 4 shows the number and size of villages in each of the four Nomoi in 1971; those in the Nomos of Iraklion tend to be larger than average, and in Lassithi, smaller:

Table 4

| Population | Khania | Number of villages | | | All Crete |
		Rethymnon	Iraklion	Lassithi	
1,000–1,999	1	2	13	2	18
500–999	24	11	54	26	115
200–499	65	53	121	39	278
50–199	250	138	126	85	599
0–49	105	44	58	100	307
0–1,999	445	248	372	252	1,317

Permanently inhabited isolated farms are very rare but there are, particularly in the more mountainous districts, almost 1,000 separate tiny communities of perhaps half a dozen to twenty families. Only eighteen villages in the whole island have populations exceeding 1,000 and these tend to be strategically placed on the outskirts of the larger towns, along the main roads and in the more prosperous agricultural districts, such as the orange-growing Apokorona of Khania and the rich vineyards of Iraklion. Since the early 1960s Greek planners concerned with the development of Crete have attempted to modify this pattern. Their aim has been to 'rationalise' the distribution of settlement by facilitating the growth of the larger- and medium-sized villages, and encouraging a pre-existing tendency on the part of the local population to move into these villages from the

RURAL LIFE, TRADITIONAL AND MODERN

smaller and more isolated mountain hamlets. In extreme cases, entire settlements have been evacuated; one such is the tiny village of Samaria, high in the White Mountains, at the head of the Samaria Gorge, and one of the few villages in Crete to have been throughout its history accessible only on foot. By abandoning such sites and concentrating investment in rural areas with some growth potential, the provision of facilities and public services has been made both speedier and a more economical operation.

FARMS AND FARMING

The great majority of the villagers are farmers. Their lands surround the villages, and individual farms are, by American and even by European standards, extremely small. The average agricultural holding is between 20 and 30 *stremmata* in area. (One *stremma* = approx $\frac{1}{4}$ acre). In the plains this may include an irrigated area of between 1 and 5 *stremmata* per holding; in the mountains, the cultivated farm area may well be much smaller than average, with the greater part of the farm income derived from grazing sheep and goats on the rockier and steeper slopes. This rough land is not enclosed, and flocks of animals are grazed on owned or rented land under the care of vigilant shepherds, with the local *agrophýlakas*, or rural guardian, settling any disputes that may arise.

The steeper cultivated hillsides are usually terraced in a series of narrow ledges, banked by stone retaining-walls. The older terraces form an intricate and irregular pattern over the hillsides; they are often accessible only on foot or by donkey, and are almost totally unsuited to mechanisation of any but the most portable kind. Quite different are the regular bench-like outlines of the modern terraces, presenting an obtrusively uniform appearance.

As one descends from the upper margins of cultivation, small irregularly shaped patches of cropland standing out among the rocks and scrub give way to an almost continuous cover of cultivated crops. The more fertile the land, the smaller field sizes tend to become. The extreme is reached in the irrigated valley floors and coastal plains where individual fields of ¼ *stremma* (1/16 acre) are not uncommon.

An individual farm holding is usually made up of several physically separate fields. The average number of plots per farm in 1963 was 10·4. Holdings of 10 and 20 *stremmata* are commonly divided into as many as fifteen to twenty plots, some very tiny and all at varying distances from each other and from the farmer's house in the village. Farming the equivalent of a 10-acre holding in Crete normally necessitates a much greater expenditure of time and effort in travelling than would be needed, say, for a 100-acre ring-fence farm in Britain. A study in 1948, when most farmers travelled to work on foot or by donkey, showed that on average 1·1 hours were added to the working day, the nearest plot being about ten minutes distant and the farthest ninety minutes. Today, improvements in transport have reduced these times for many, but planners still frequently lament the loss of work-time and forget, perhaps, that a typical London or New York commuter may spend as much as two hours per day getting to and from work.

The fragmented character of the Cretan farm, although apparently and in some ways actually inefficient, has also its advantages. In the pre-war days of subsistence peasant farming, when a farmer's choice of crops was determined as far as possible by his family's food requirements, it made good sense to have land with a variety of physical characteristics; this usually meant working land in several different parts of the village's territory. The fortunate farmer was one who had a little valley bottom land for the cultivation of irrigated fruit and vegetables, some hill land for cereals, olives, vines, and fodder crops, and some rough grazing for his animals. The farmer with a single block of land was restricted in the range of crops he could grow, and was much more vulnerable to natural disasters, such as flooding or destructive hailstorms. Furthermore, following traditional inheritance and dowry customs, land was and often still is divided between heirs, and frequently forms all or part of a girl's dowry when she marries. Given the continuance of these practices, consolidated holdings have little chance of survival beyond the span of a single generation.

Land fragmentation, inheritance and dowry customs are an integral part of the peasant way of life; they have been established over the centuries with one principal underlying objective: to give maximum security to the members of the farm family. Seen from this viewpoint, the system has much to recommend it. For a progressive farmer of the present generation, however, its structures are often too confining to permit the efficient application of many modern farming methods.

Cretan agriculture exists at present in a state of compromise; many elements of traditional subsistence farming survive, but an increasing number of farmers are switching to cash crops and risking greater specialisation. Out of a total cultivated area of 3 million *stremmata*, cereals occupy just over one-third and olive groves just under one-third. Half of the remaining 1 million *stremmata* is devoted to vineyards and the remainder to a wide range of minor crops, such as vegetables, citrus fruits, melons, carobs and other tree crops.

Vines

Although not occupying the largest area, vines contribute more than any other crop group to the value of total crop production—753 million drachmae in 1963, as against 543 million from olives and 275 million from cereals. The vineyards serve a variety of purposes, and wine-making—their main traditional use—is still important. Many farmers make their own wine and there is a growing number of wine-making co-operatives and private companies who produce a wide range of wines, spirits and liqueurs. The wines are mostly drunk very young and vary enormously in quality. This variation, which is not normally found in the main commercial brands, is largely due to the fact that there are many small producers, each with his own customs and standards, and also to the existence in Crete of a large number of different cultivated varieties of wine grape.

CRETE

Sieber, in 1817, noticed over sixty varieties. Although one of these, the Aliático, is of good quality, the rest are only poor or mediocre. Improvements are being made, with the introduction of proved varieties from France and elsewhere, and also in the reorganisation of wine-production methods. Progress is retarded, however, by the fact that not since the Venetian period has wine-making been regarded by Cretan farmers as an important money earner.

In the fourteenth and fifteenth centuries Malvoisie, or Malmsey, was the island's principal export, with records of regular sales as far afield as Germany, England and Poland; in 1576 Cretan wines were taken by the Portuguese on their journeys to the East Indies. Boschini, writing during the siege of Iraklion by the Turks, mentioned that Rethymnon alone exported 12,000 pipes of wine annually—about $1\frac{1}{4}$ million gallons. Wine production appears to have declined under the Moslem Turks and gradually to have become geared to home needs rather than those of international markets. Too often today considerations of quality are ignored, and the fermentation vats sometimes receive a mixture of wine grapes and unsuitable grapes, such as surplus sultana and table grapes.

To the commercially minded farmer, the best prospects for viticulture lie in the more specialised and labour-intensive production of early table grapes and sultanas. In their present form both are relatively new cash crops in Crete. Sultana-growing, in spite of world market problems, has remained important since its popularisation in the 1920s by Greek immigrants from Asia Minor. Technological innovations in the packing, preserving and transporting of fresh produce, and the skilled breeding of new early varieties, have led to a large increase in the area under table grapes, particularly near Iraklion. Much of the green and fertile appearance of the island is due to the large spread of vineyards on the lower hill slopes. Some of the vines are grown in a low, bushy form; others, particularly the sultana and table grapes, are carefully trained up trellises. When seen from a distance in the summer they appear as a raised carpet of bright green; in the winter they form an intricate interlacing of branches.

Olives

The second most important branch of farming by value is the cultivation of olives. Of the estimated total of 17 million trees (1966), the majority are grown in regular, planted groves and the remainder scattered over a wide area. Almost all the olives are used for oil production rather than for sale as table olives. The harvest, usually regarded mainly as women's work, takes place in the winter months and the olives are gathered by beating the branches. Yields fluctuate, but in a good year a crop of over 100,000 tons of olives may be obtained. At its best, a single tree can produce enough olives to yield 20kg (44lb) of oil when pressed. After pressing, the olive residue is compressed into briquettes which provide a cheap, slow-burning fuel used, for example, in many bakers' ovens.

The olive is an undemanding tree; it thrives with careful cultivation, pruning, irrigation and pest control, but it can also exist untended on remote rocky hillsides where the rainfall may be as low as 380mm (15in) a year. Today, the olive is most competitive economically in frost-free, fertile, semi-mountainous areas with a high rainfall. In the past olives, often intercropped with cereals, also covered the plains, flourishing in the deep fertile soils. With the recent expansion of irrigated cash crops in these areas, the olives have given place to citrus, vegetables and bananas. In the Khania district, the change-over may sometimes be seen in mixed orchards where mature olive trees alternate with young, newly planted orange trees; the olives remain temporarily, to guarantee an income until the orange trees become productive. Although olive cultivation is contracting in many of the most fertile areas, it still remains important in parts of the Messara Plain. Together with wheat, the olive holds a special place in the affections of many farmers for whose ancestors these crops have been staples for over 5,000 years.

CRETE

Cereals

For well over a century, Crete has needed to supplement her cereal production by importing grain; earlier, however, she regularly exported large quantities of cheap grain to Rome and Venice. Most famous was the wheat produced in the Messara Plain, which was the best quality of any in the island and won an honourable mention as late as 1855 at the great World Exhibition in Paris. Today, although no longer significant for export, cereal cultivation is still important to many farmers; a 1965 study of the village of Pobia in the Messara Plain showed that most farmers, although well aware of more profitable alternatives, still preferred to grow enough wheat to meet their family's needs for flour.

Other crops

Although as yet small in acreage, the production of vegetables is expanding rapidly. By taking advantage of Crete's southerly position and warm climate, fresh vegetables can be produced out of season for marketing in north European countries. Intensive production methods are used, including irrigation and cultivation under temporary polythene greenhouses, which are becoming a feature of the Messara Plain and some of the smaller coastal plains. The most important of the many crops that are grown are tomatoes and cucumbers.

Crete is not a major producer of industrial crops, although there is a small area of cotton. More important locally are speciality crops, such as peanuts near Rethymnon, bananas from Mallia, chestnuts in western Crete, almonds from Neapolis, and apples and pears from Lassithi. Carob or locust beans grow widely and, although no longer greatly harvested, were once an important export crop; in 1937, for example, Crete produced about 26,000 tons of carob beans, of which almost half was exported, mostly to France. Under Turkish rule, tobacco was widely grown and, throughout the days of self-sufficiency, flax was a common crop and much silk was produced.

RURAL LIFE, TRADITIONAL AND MODERN

Animal husbandry
The total crop area of Crete amounts to only three-eighths of the total land area; the remainder is unsuitable for cultivation of any kind. It is this land, with its uncompromising stony mountain slopes, that serves as pasture for the ¾ million sheep and goats (741,377 in 1966), which scramble amongst the rocks, conducting a vigilant patrol through the garrigue in a life-long search for food. Little is done to ease their task by improving and maintaining the pastures; indeed in some areas serious over-grazing has caused deterioration, as the vegetation has become dominated by unpalatable spiny plants and shrubs.

Pasture in Crete is owned publicly by the communes and privately by individuals, with a small area belonging to the monasteries. Although virtually none of the pasture is fenced, the grazing of flocks upon particular areas of land is very closely regulated and controlled. The high mountain pastures can only be used in summer; in winter they are covered in snow and the flocks move down to more sheltered lowland grazing. Thus a seasonal pattern of movement takes place, often following long-established routes to traditional grazing grounds. The patterns of land and flock ownership, and the renting of pasture, are often extremely complex. A highland stock-owner may have his own winter grazing; he may rent it at preferential rates from his commune or at higher rates from a neighbouring farmer or commune, or he may have to seek summer grazing in the lowland, far from his home and at a high rent. Rent must also be paid for the right of passage or access across another man's land. Many flock owners have no pasture of their own, and many landowners have no flocks; it is in such circumstances that agreements may be made which can easily lead to pasture deterioration. The landowner seeks a high rent and the stock-owner, particularly if he has made only a short-term agreement, uses the land at maximum carrying capacity.

By the end of the long dry summer many of the flocks are in an under-nourished state. Very few farmers give their animals

CRETE

any supplementary feed, and both ewes and she-goats have low milk yields of about 50kg (110lb) a year. They tend also to be small animals, giving about 7kg (15lb) of marketed meat. Local breeds of sheep include the Sphakia, Psiloriti and Zagros or Lassithi. All are well adjusted to their active life, but the Sphakia type is perhaps the best prospect commercially, being larger and heavier than the others and having a higher milk yield.

In addition to the $\frac{1}{2}$ million flock animals, there are a further $\frac{1}{4}$ million domestic sheep and goats (239,328 in 1966), approximately three per farm family. The élite of the caprine world, most of these domestic animals lead a life of luxury. Treasured and cosseted by their owners, they shelter under the family roof by night, and by day, towed in the wake of the youngest or oldest member of the family, they are led out to the best grazing. In return, these animals provide enough milk to meet the family's requirements for dairy products, such as milk, cheese and yogurt.

Although some cheese is still made in the home, commercial production has long been in the hands of specialists. Old stone-built circular cheesehouses, although no longer used, can still be seen on the northern slopes of Psiloriti. Here solitary shepherds once stored and slowly matured their cheeses on cool stone shelves. Today the milk is taken down to the towns, to small family premises and larger modern factories, such as that at Rethymnon, where the smooth yogurt, the soft moist *mizíthra*, the *graviéra* and other hard Cretan cheeses are made.

THE CRETAN DIET

The diet of the country people has changed relatively little in the last 4,000 years; then as now it was closely tied to the local range of food crops and to their seasonal availability. In Minoan Crete, the main staples were cereal grains for bread-making, and olives, with beans, wild greens, herbs and fruits in season. There were also limited quantities of fish, meat and milk products. The

RURAL LIFE, TRADITIONAL AND MODERN

cultivation of the vine was introduced to Crete some 3,000 years ago, and more recent additions in the last 1,000 years have been citrus fruits, tomatoes, potatoes, maize, bananas and peanuts.

Today the range of foods available to the rural population through cultivation and purchase is very great, but the main staples remain unchanged. No meal is complete without bread, which has a deep-rooted symbolic significance for many Cretans, in addition to its more practical dietetic role. Other important sources of carbohydrate are potatoes, spaghetti and rice. Olives and olive oil provide a major source of energy with the average annual consumption of olive oil being about 18kg (40lb) per person. In addition to being used freely as a cooking oil, it is poured over salads and often added to soups and cooked vegetables. Animal fats and butter are used only in small amounts.

The pattern of vegetable consumption, unlike that of olive oil and bread, varies considerably from season to season. Those vegetables which cannot be readily preserved and stored are consumed fresh in large quantities, particularly during the summer and early autumn months. Various green leafy vegetables, beans, squash, eggplants, okra, artichokes, green peppers, tomatoes and cucumbers are among the most popular. During the winter months fewer fresh vegetables, such as cabbage and onions, are available, and the emphasis is upon various varieties of beans, lentils and split peas which can be preserved in dried form until required. Tomato paste is commonly used as an ingredient of the savoury soups, stews and herb-flavoured sauces in which these vegetables are cooked, but only small use is made of tinned vegetables.

There is a Greek saying that 'Pulses are the poor man's meat' and, although meat consumption is increasing in Crete, as in Greece as a whole, it remains a relatively small constituent of the diet. Lamb, veal, kid, beef and pork are all available, lamb being the most common, but meat has always been relatively expensive and regarded as an occasional luxury. In most households, however, meat becomes a major item on the menu for

CRETE

special occasions, such as times of family celebration, feast days and holidays. The meat intake is normally supplemented by a high consumption of chickens, particularly following the introduction of intensive poultry production in the late 1960s.

Fresh fish, like meat, is expensive to buy but, unlike meat (with the exception of corned beef), is available in a wide variety of tinned and preserved forms of which dried, salted cod, herrings, anchovies and tinned sardines are the most important. Popular fresh fish are red and grey mullet, bream, sinagrídha (*Dentex dentex*), sphyrídha (*Epinephelus aeneus*), prawns, lobster, squid and octopus.

The protein content of the Cretan diet is extensively supplemented by a large variety of dairy products, of which numerous cheeses and yogurts made from sheep and goats' milk are the most important. Fruits are eaten in season, with fresh oranges at their best during the winter months and spring, and grapes during the late summer and autumn. Other important fruits include melons from the irrigated plains, and apples, pears, plums and cherries from the mountains, together with pomegranates, figs, apricots, peaches, quinces, bananas and prickly pear fruits. Certain fruits, such as figs and sultanas, are dried and others preserved in candied form or in syrup. Sugar is imported from the mainland and is used in addition to the traditional home-produced sweetener, honey. Both are used in a wide variety of confections, cakes, puddings and sweet pastries.

RURAL INDUSTRIES

As communications improve and the impact of the outside world on the Cretans has become stronger and more insistent, the role of the home and local craftsmen has become smaller and less important. Even the limited industrialisation which has come to the island has made the practising of many trades on a purely village basis uneconomic. In cases such as wine-making and flour-milling, where power-driven machinery has been introduced, the smallest viable unit has become too large for an

13 A peasant woman rides to work in the fields

14 *(above)* an animal-powered chain pump drawing water from a shallow well on the coastal plain near Rethymnon; *(below)* a woman of Anoyia winding wool on to a shuttle, while waiting to sell her handwoven rugs

RURAL LIFE, TRADITIONAL AND MODERN

individual in a village to operate, and then the trade tends to be taken over either by a cooperative or by an urban-based entrepreneur.

Wine-making and distilling

The making of wine has now become one of the most important and most technologically sophisticated industries. Almost every family has some land on which grapes are grown and makes some wine at home. Most of the Cretan wine which comes on the open market, however, is made in industrial plants which belong either to cooperatives, as at Peza and Sitia; to individuals, such as Miliarákis and Mathioudákis at Iraklion; or to commercial enterprises, such as VIOCHYM at Khania. The output of the larger production units is measured in hundreds of tons per year, and the wine is subject at every stage in its production to rigorous chemical and biological controls.

Formerly almost every village had its distillery, but now stills (*kazánia*) are mostly confined to the towns. The products range from unflavoured pure grape spirit—*rakí*, the arrack of eighteenth-century England—through *oúzo* and brandy to passable imitations of French liqueurs sold under such names as Benedictine and Triple Sec. *Raki*, also known as *tsípouro* and *tsikoudiá*, and *ouzo* are distilled from the residue left after wine making, in much the same way as *marc* is made in Burgundy. *Ouzo* is flavoured by re-distillation in the presence of anise and other aromatic seeds. Brandy, called *koniak* in Greek, is distilled from wine; that made by the better firms is of good quality, although different in character from the French *cognac*.

Since the sultana grape was introduced into Crete in the 1920s it has become almost a monoculture in parts of the Nomos of Iraklion and in the irrigated Pantelis valley at Sitia. The grapes, of the variety known as *sultanína*, are harvested and sun-dried by the growers. They are then sold either to merchants who pack and export them or to the government, which buys at a supported minimum price. Those bought by the government are warehoused until the world price makes it profitable to sell them. This price is fixed annually by agreement between the main producing countries of Greece, Turkey, the USA and Australia.

Olive oil producing

Few Cretan villages are without an olive oil mill; sometimes there are several, one of which may be operated by an agricultural cooperative, and others by private individuals. Concentration into large units remote from the areas of production is impracticable and it has remained essentially a village industry. The quality of the oil is rapidly spoiled by delay between the harvesting and the processing of the olives. Also, olives are harvested on a family basis, and hence become available for processing in a succession of small batches rather than in a continuous stream.

Before the rise of the cooperatives, the pressing of olives was frequently done by the producers themselves. Hand-operated screw presses were used in the smaller installations, and donkey-powered pan-mills with edge-stones in the larger. An installation consisting of a screw press and a pan-mill in the same building can be seen at the uninhabited monastery of Ayios Ioannis on Akrotiri. Screw presses are often to be found outside farms in olive-producing country. Modern practice is tending towards the use of hydraulic presses, and these are being manufactured by a firm in Khania, as well as in mainland Greece.

When the export price of olive oil is too low to afford a profit to the producers, the oil is bought at a fixed price by the state. The tanks in which this oil is stored are conspicuous in several areas of olive oil production as, for example, in Sitia.

Flour-milling

Flour-milling in Crete is an agricultural processing industry which has, in the last century, totally changed in technology, location, and scale of production units. Relics of a former age are the large, stone-built, tower windmills still to be found, particularly in the eastern part of the island. They stand imposingly

RURAL LIFE, TRADITIONAL AND MODERN

in rows on many of the more considerable cols and interfluves, but occasionally a solitary mill may be seen, as at the monastery of Toplou, east of Sitia. Tower mills were still operating during the first half of this century, but nearly all are now derelict, often roofless and with their timber and iron working parts removed.

Windmills were supplemented by a considerable number of small, privately owned water-mills. These occur throughout the island and are frequently found in flights of up to seven mills, each re-using the same water. They are nearly all of the same type, having a horizontal water wheel, and are relatively sophisticated developments of an ancient and primitive watermill once found in Britain and much of Europe, but now only to be seen in the Balkans, Turkey and farther east.

In Crete, the mills are supplied with stream or spring water via leets or diversion channels to a point some way above the mill buildings. Where only a small quantity of water is available, a mill may have its own tiny reservoir in which the water can be accumulated until required. From the reservoir or direct from the leet, the water is led out away from the hillside in a short horizontal channel, at the end of which it falls through an almost vertical chute, down to the mill. The water passes down behind the first floor of the mill building, and shoots horizontally through a nozzle placed in the back wall of the ground floor. The jet of water hits the blades of a wooden or metal horizontal wheel, causing it to rotate and drive the mill stone which is located above in the first floor. Such mills were small and slow, but could be relied upon whenever water was available. Although no longer in use, they were still working in the more remote parts of the island as recently as 1958.

Mills driven by wind or water were made almost immediately obsolete when, first the oil engine and, in 1965, the public electricity supply became generally available. Milling then developed into a more centralised industry. This trend has been fostered by the growth of the larger towns and the improvement of the ports and road system. The island now relies for its flour to an increasing extent on imported wheat processed in large milling units at the ports of Iraklion and Soudha. Production at Soudha is to be extended to include animal feeding-stuffs. This will improve the position of the dairy and meat producers who are not able to increase production significantly without imported animal food. It could also have the effect of halting the decline in the number of cattle in Crete, particularly if dairying becomes a local growth industry, as poultry farming did in the 1960s.

Spinning and weaving

In 1948, 60 per cent of all Cretan households practised spinning and 43 per cent did their own weaving. Today these percentages are much reduced and the domestic textile industry survives mainly in a fragmented form in a few rural households, being more specialised and concentrated in one or two mountain villages, such as Anoyia. Here the main strength of the village economy is animal husbandry, and many of the villagers have developed the associated traditional arts of spinning, weaving and crochet-work to meet the demands of the tourist industry. Their products are sold to the tourist shops in the main cities, and visitors to the village are offered a brightly coloured motley of rugs, shoulder bags and shawls. These are made from the local natural wool, dyed with imported dyes, and woven into a variety of abstract, geometrical and pictorial designs, mostly non-traditional and geared to the supposed taste of the international tourist.

Charcoal-burning

In the countryside, wood was the chief domestic fuel, used by 91 per cent of rural households in 1948. Most if it was burnt in the form of brushwood, the larger branches being reserved for the charcoal burner. In the towns, charcoal was used by over half of all households as compared with only 6 per cent of rural households. Since then, charcoal as a domestic fuel has been replaced by bottled gas, except in many restaurants and for the

RURAL LIFE, TRADITIONAL AND MODERN

public and ceremonial roasting of whole carcasses, as in the village of Drosiá (Yeni Gavé). To meet the residual demand for charcoal for cooking and blacksmithing, a few wood-colliers continue to practise their ancient craft. Their kilns may occasionally be seen by the roadside in clearings between the trees. They are neat conical mounds built up from straight branches of trees something over a metre in length; the mound is some 2–2½ metres (7ft) in diameter and about the same height. It is covered by a thin layer of clay or soil, 5–6cm (2in) thick, having a series of holes at ground level around its circumference. These holes are just the right size to admit enough air for slow and incomplete combustion of the wood, and a further hole, at the apex of the cone, lets out the smoke. The interior of the cone contains small sticks which burn and provide the heat to carbonise the larger ones on the periphery.

Lime-burning

Although lime mortar has been replaced in modern building construction by the use of Portland cement, the lime kiln is still a familiar feature in the countryside. The raw material is readily available in most parts of the island and the kilns are fired by olive residue. The lime is used for lime-washing the exteriors of houses and churches, for plastering and for rough and traditional building. A few lime burners, as at Iraklion and Ayios Nikolaos, operate their own trucks to collect their raw materials and to distribute their products.

TRADITIONAL CRAFTS

Despite the changes in rural life brought about by developments in communications and in technology, some traditional trades are still carried on in the villages and towns. One of these is the craft of the saddle-maker, whose skill is unlikely to die out while farmers continue to make their way via mountain paths to cultivate remote and relatively inaccessible fields. The village saddle-maker is not only a skilled wood-worker, but also

CRETE

works in leather to make the thick pads on which the saddle rests.

The pack animals also need shoes which are made to a pattern resembling the ancient Roman horse-shoe. The shoe-smiths operate from the larger villages and towns, and each smith serves the farmers from several villages.

Part of the traditional dress of Cretan men is a pair of polished, hand-made leather knee-boots; the custom of wearing these has largely continued, though other features of traditional costume, such as the baggy trousers, are only occasionally seen. Not only are knee-boots practical in the countryside, but they have become an accepted part of modern country dress while working and for more formal occasions. Thus for many years to come the boot-makers will continue to be a feature of the towns, at work in the doors of their shops, cutting the leather, shaping it on wooden lasts and sewing it to make the tough supple boots their customers demand.

Traditional method of threshing

10 THE TOWNS AND URBAN LIFE

THE population of Crete amounts to almost ½ million people—456,642 in 1971; of these, well over half (68 per cent) live in the 1,317 villages scattered throughout the island, and the remainder in the eighteen 'urban' settlements—that is, with a population exceeding 2,000. By European standards, these are very small and the fifteen settlements at the lower end of the urban spectrum, with 2,000–10,000 inhabitants, vary in character and function from overgrown villages acting as very local service centres, such as Krítsa (Lassithi), to small but cosmopolitan urban centres functioning as regional capitals, such as Ayios Nikolaos. Others, like Tymbaki and Mires in the Messara Plain, have more the appearance and atmosphere of small boom towns.

URBAN CENTRES

As a simple form of classification, settlements in the 2,000–4,999 population range are described as local centres; 5,000–9,999 as small urban centres, and 10,000 plus as large urban centres. Table 5 clearly shows the dominance over all other urban centres of the two main cities: Iraklion and Khania. There is a large gap between the smaller of the two, Khania, with a population of 45,531, and the third largest town, Rethymnon, with just under 15,000. Only three other towns on the island—Ierapetra, Sitia and Ayios Nikolaos—have over 5,000 inhabitants; these are in the Nomos of Lassithi at the eastern end of the island. Here—unlike central and western Crete, where the one major city forms the administrative capital in each

CRETE

Table 5

POPULATION OF URBAN SETTLEMENTS (1971)

Large urban centres	
Greater Iraklion	83,691
(includes Nea Alikarnassos)	
Greater Khania	45,531
(includes Soudha)	
Rethymnon	14,969
3 large urban centres:	*144,191*
Small urban centres	
Ierapetra (Nomos of Lassithi)	7,055
Sitia (Lassithi)	6,176
Ayios Nikolaos (Lassithi)	5,002
3 small urban centres:	*18,233*
Local centres	
Arkhanes (Iraklion)	3,523
Tymbaki (Iraklion)	3,229
Mournies (Khania)	3,134
Neapolis (Lassithi)	3,070
Kastelli (Khania)	2,996
Mires (Iraklion)	2,948
Anoyia (Rethymnon)	2,750
Kroussón (Iraklion)	2,676
Zaros (Iraklion)	2,135
Arkalokhori (Iraklion)	2,121
Nerokouros (Khania)	2,077
Kritsa (Lassithi)	2,015
12 local centres:	*32,674*
Total	*195,098*

Source: National Statistical Service of Greece: *Population of Greece at the Census of 14 March 1971* (Athens, 1972)

Nomos—there is no one large and clearly dominant urban centre. One of the small urban centres, Ayios Nikolaos, forms the regional capital and the only other urban settlements are

THE TOWNS AND URBAN LIFE

local centres of vastly different character. Kritsa is merely a large though attractive village, which has prospered with the coming of the film industry to Crete, whereas Neapolis has a true urban character. Formerly a village, in 1868 one of the governors of Lassithi, a vigorous and respected reformer known as Adhosidhis Kostis Pasha, made it his administrative capital. He laid out a new town with avenues, squares, gardens and impressive public buildings, and appropriately, named it Neapolis. In spite of local protests, the capital was transferred to Ayios Nikolaos in 1904, although Neapolis remains the seat of the Petra bishopric and the principal law courts of the region.

There has been a six-fold increase in the size of the major towns in just over a century. In common with the greater part of the inhabited world, Crete has been experiencing its own urban explosion. The overall growth rate of the island's population has been around 5 per cent per decade from 1941 to 1961, while the equivalent growth rate in the main towns averaged 22·7 per cent. Thus the combined population of the three principal cities rose from 83,399 in 1940 to 124,661 in 1961; and by 1971 it had risen to 144,191. The bulk of the increase derives from the rural areas, as a steady stream of school-leavers and younger men move off the land into the towns, to be followed at a later date by their families and sometimes also by other relatives.

A glance at the map of Crete shows that all the large urban centres and administrative capitals lie on the northern coast. They are linked by the island's main artery, the north coast road, surrounded by rich coastal plains and backed by poor mountainous hinterlands. For thousands of years these ports have been the economic pivot of Crete, providing domestic links within the island and forming the termini of vital trade and administrative links across the Cretan Sea northwards to Greece, Venice, Turkey and Constantinople. The cities growing up round the ports have dominated the economic life of the island as centres of trade, industry, finance and administration.

CRETE

In spite of the more recent decline of coastal shipping round Crete, the main towns have expanded their role as regional service centres following the great improvements made in road transport. Each of the four regional capitals is the headquarters of its own extensive and efficient bus service and each town is served by an extensive road network. Each year there is a large increase in the number of road vehicles of all types carrying produce and passengers to the markets and shops. The main towns also contain small-scale industries, banking and specialised services, tourist facilities and social attractions, such as cafés, restaurants, open-air and indoor cinemas, and night clubs.

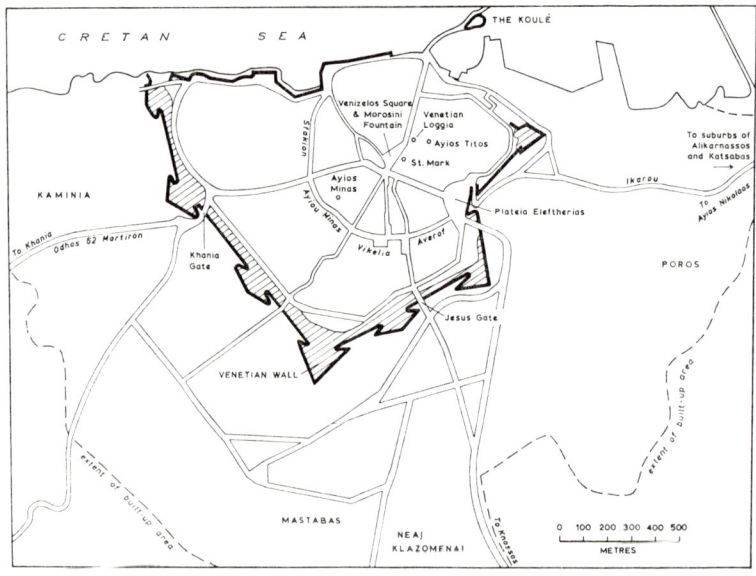

Iraklion: old city and modern suburbs

IRAKLION

The limits of the medieval city are still sharply defined by the massive Venetian walls encircling the landward side of the small knoll on which the town is built. Beyond the walls to the south,

THE TOWNS AND URBAN LIFE

west and east extend the modern suburbs of the city; to the north lie the harbours and the sea. The fortifications of Iraklion, together with its churches, are its most interesting historical features. The town had been fortified since its foundation by the Arabs in AD 824, but by the mid-fifteenth century it had outgrown its Byzantine walls, which probably ran along the line of the present-day streets of Sfakión, Áyiou Mínas, Vikéla and Avérof, and had spread beyond them to form a semi-circle of extra-mural suburbs (see map).

When, after the fall of Constantinople in 1453, the need arose once more to make the city defensible, the Venetians planned a new line of walls completely enclosing what was then the full extent of their capital. The construction of the new defences was a massive operation in every sense, beginning in 1462 and taking more than a century to complete. Their effectiveness was finally demonstrated at the time of the Turkish invasion when, for twenty-two years, the city held out alone against the Turks.

Along its 3-kilometre length, the wall is massively high and thick with a rubble-filled core faced with dressed stone and strengthened at intervals by seven bastions of a characteristic flat arrowhead shape. Of the four original Venetian gates, two now survive: the Pantókrator or Khania Gate, the Pórta Khanión, to the west, and the Jesus or New Gate, the Kenoúria Pórta, to the south. Both these gates are now in the care of the Archaeological Service and are being restored. The Harbour Gate, through which the city was approached from the harbour, was destroyed in 1898 when Admiral Noel bombarded the city after the Turks murdered the British Consul. To the east of the city, a steep road with two hairpin bends leads directly into the great square called Platéia Eleftherías, where the inhabitants stroll on summer evenings in the ritual of the *vólta*. To create this square, named in commemoration of the liberation of Crete from the Turks, the Venetian gate of Áyios Geórgios, commonly called the Lazaretto Gate, was pulled down between 1913 and 1917. The gate is remembered only in the name of a nearby bus-stop: Trís Kamáres (Three Arches).

Only about a quarter of the full extent of modern Iraklion lies within the Venetian walls. The old town today contains the main business district and shopping streets of the city, the street market, and the principal churches, squares, public buildings and hotels, together with some of the older residential areas. Architecturally, it forms a great mixture of styles and periods, but with relatively little surviving from Venetian times or earlier. During World War II, 30 per cent of all the buildings in the city were destroyed, including many of great historical interest and many private homes. As late as 1948, about 200 of the families who had lost their homes were still living in caves on the outskirts of Iraklion, and many others were sheltered in temporary homes in outlying districts.

Iraklion is subject to frequent and occasionally severe earthquakes. Two exceedingly destructive shocks have occurred during the last century, with serious damage as recently as 1926 and 1931, and minor damage in 1969. The 1926 earthquake was described by Elliadhi, the British Vice-Consul in Iraklion at the time:

> I was sitting with my wife in a café near the old Venetian fountain, when at about ten pm, we felt the first indications of a shock. Thinking that it would be one of the light shocks to which we are accustomed, we did not leave our seats at once. But noticing that the commotion continued, and that liquor and other bottles commenced falling from the shelves round about us, we all rushed to the door and stood in the open, close to the Venetian fountain, whilst the shocks continued. At this critical moment the electric light was cut off, for fear of fires through short-circuits, so we were left in the darkness to hear a terrific crash, and find ourselves enveloped in dust through the collapse of three shops close by.... As most of the houses suffered more or less from this shock, a large part of the inhabitants passed more than one night in the open air for fear of other shocks.

Probably the oldest surviving features of Iraklion, apart from its site, are its street pattern and harbour. Even where the original buildings have gone, the streets have followed their same course for centuries. Paved streets are a comparatively new innovation in Iraklion. Xanthoudidis, writing in 1925, says that at that time the thoroughfares were a welter of mud and dust, and this state of affairs continued at least until 1935. Xanthoudidis contrasts the streets of his time with those of the Turkish era remembered by his older fellow-citizens—when 'the roads were paved with stone and the footpaths were laid with little white and black pebbles made into patterns of trees'.

The older residential areas within the walls, such as that in the south-east corner, comprise a maze of narrow streets fronted by tightly packed houses most of which are Turkish in construction. Many have the characteristic projecting first and second storeys and large wooden shutters; some have balconies and vine-shaded courtyards and small gardens, enclosed by high walls. In other areas, most of the old houses have gone, and new bright white-washed concrete blocks of flats and houses have taken their place.

In the centre of the city, urban renewal has taken place along many of the main streets; shops and offices have been modernised, and sites cleared for government buildings and large hotels, so that much of the face of old Iraklion has disappeared. The very size and massiveness of the Venetian wall has ensured its survival, although in some places many of the dressed facing stones have been quarried and re-used in other buildings—a practice the Venetians themselves had followed when, in building the wall, they used stone from the Minoan sites of Knossos and Amnissos. Until quite recently, the eastern and southern parts of the wide ditch were filled with a makeshift jumble of squatters' houses. The inhabitants of these have now been re-housed in a new estate on the south-western edge of the city; the ditch has been turned into a sports area and ornamental garden and, in summer, part of it is used as an open-air cinema.

Down on the seafront, the small Venetian harbour still survives as a refuge for fishing boats, pleasure craft and other small

CRETE

vessels. A low, early sixteenth-century fort (Koulé), marked with the winged lion of Venice, still guards the entrance, but is now outflanked by new concrete moles, as the Venetian ship-sheds on the landward side are over-topped by many-storeyed hotels. East of the Venetian harbour lies the new harbour, begun in the inter-war period and subsequently extended. The low-lying land behind has become an industrial zone, separated both from the old city to the west and the newer suburbs sited on higher ground to the south.

Other industries in Iraklion, consisting mainly of agricultural processing and small-scale engineering, are located in various parts of the town, such as the Street of the 62 Martyrs (Ódhos 62 Martíron) just outside the Khania Gate, which contains many small metal-working and engineering firms. The size of most industrial establishments, particularly of those industries not based on agricultural raw materials, is noticeably small. In 1932, Elliadhi dismissed the industries of Iraklion as 'not worth mentioning'; even today, most are small family firms employing fewer than five workers. However, there is no simple relationship in Cretan industry between size and efficiency. A 1948 study of eleven sultana factories indicated a range in daily output from 6 to 60 tons per eight-hour day; the number of employees ranged from 8 to 360 per factory, and horsepower from 18 to 110. One of the smaller factories produced each ton of sultanas with the same amount of power but only one-sixth of the labour required by two of the larger factories.

The Street of the 62 Martyrs and also Iákarou, a street with a number of metal-working establishments on the east side of the city, form part of the great extra-mural development which has taken place during the last half-century. The city is spreading out over an ever-increasing area to the south, west and east. On the east side, new suburbs have been built at Poros and as far as the Nea Alikarnassos. Development in this direction will be restricted by the presence of the airfield and by the rough and rocky terrain. To the south, the main urban sprawl stops at Mastabás and Neai Klazomenai, but a ribbon development of

THE TOWNS AND URBAN LIFE

villas extends as far as Néa Fortétsa and almost to Knossos. To the west, the suburbs spread less far and are regarded as being socially less desirable. However, the character of the area may change once the effect is felt of the National Road and other recent developments.

Historic monuments

Travelling into the centre of the city, the visitor who seeks some monuments to 700 years of Venetian and Turkish rule will not be entirely disappointed. The Venetians built seventeen Latin churches in Iraklion, most of them larger than the Orthodox ones. Many have been destroyed by earthquakes, but that of St Mark, built by the Venetian colonists in 1239, has been restored and is used as a cultural centre. The tower, lost during the Turkish occupation, was replaced by a minaret; the church itself, like many in Crete, was used as a mosque until 1915. Almost opposite to it, across Venizélos Square, formerly the Venetian corn market, stood the Ducal Palace. Only a few arcades of this building survive, sheltering small shops, some of which sell souvenirs.

Two of the most striking monuments of Venetian rule now remaining were built by the *Proveditor General* Francesco Morosini. The more famous of these is the marble Lion Fountain in the centre of Venizelos Square. This first began to flow on St Mark's Day (25 April) 1628 with water supplied from an aqueduct, also built by Morosini. The other is the so-called Venetian Loggia which stands at the north-east corner of the square, at the top of 25 August Street. Built in 1626–8, it served as a kind of club for the senior Venetian officials of the city. The Turks used it as an office, and later earthquakes and acts of official vandalism almost destroyed it. Various efforts were made from 1900 onwards to restore it; rebuilding finally began in the 1960s, and was completed in the early 1970s.

The Venetians, while undoubtedly great builders, were also destroyers of much that was earlier and valuable in the Cretan heritage. Some of the damage and devastation caused in and around Iraklion during the early years of the Venetian occupation are described in a Memorandum presented by the 'Bishops, Abbots, Priests and People of Handax' to the Doge of Venice in about 1224. They thank the Doge for sending them the good Domenico Davanzago as Duke, in contrast to the Duke Curino, who called them 'dogs and Devils' and did no justice by them. Curino, they said, had laid waste the city and its suburbs, had driven away 30,000 of the inhabitants and had pulled down their houses. Hardly 200 people remained in the city, and the damage done amounted to 400,000 marks. The Venetians were not the only destructive force at work in medieval Iraklion. It is recorded that an earthquake in 1330 completely destroyed the city and that a plague which followed it killed most of the inhabitants.

Of the Byzantine town and the Arab fort very little remains. The changing history of Iraklion's Byzantine cathedral of Áyios Títos illustrates the historical vicissitudes of the city and of the island as a whole. Starting life under the protection of Byzantium, it became under the Venetians in AD 1204 the Cathedral of the Latin (Roman) archbishop. Like its more famous counterpart Áyia Sophía, in Constantinople, it was equipped with minarets and converted into a mosque following the capture of the city by the Turks. In 1856 it was destroyed by an earthquake and rebuilt, remaining a mosque until the 1920s when the minaret was pulled down and the building returned to the Church of Crete and re-dedicated. The present cathedral church is the much larger and more magnificent Áyios Mínas, built at the end of the nineteenth century.

Echoes of these earlier periods of Iraklion's history survive in some of the local place-names. The city centre, near the traffic lights and the policeman, is still called by its Arabic name, *mejdan*. When the Byzantines recovered Crete they sometimes called the city Megálo Kástro, the Large Castle, or just Kastro. This is still used in conversation by the modern inhabitants, who call themselves Kastriní. The Crusaders and other Franks called the place Candia, a name used indiscriminately

15 *(above)* Ayios Nikolaos: part of the town, showing the main bus station and, on the hill above, the imposing administrative centre of the Nomos of Lassithi; *(below)* a street in the mountain village of Anoyia, totally rebuilt after World War II

16 Ayios Nikolaos: *(above)* fishermen repair their nets beside the harbour; *(below)* the harbour, showing the bridge over the entrance to the inner lake

THE TOWNS AND URBAN LIFE

by the Venetians for the city and for the whole island. These names survived under the Turks and the name Iraklion, as the city is now officially known, only came into use after 1821.

In the first century BC, Strabo regarded Iraklion simply as the port of Knossos and, to distinguish it from other similarly named places, he called it the Knossian Iraklion. Today's tourists, who disembark at Iraklion merely to take a bus to Knossos and back, probably think of the place much as Strabo did. To those prepared to give it more time, Iraklion has much to offer in return. Apart from its walls and old streets, there are a number of individual buildings which are worth searching out, and a constant liveliness and bustling activity in its commercial districts. The Kastrini, who are noted throughout the island for their business acumen and their devotion to the art of making money, are no less warm-hearted and hospitable than other Cretans.

KHANIA

Khania, the ancient Kydonia, traditional home of quinces, has throughout its known history been a city of some consequence. It was famous in Homer's time and later rivalled Knossos and Gortys in power. Of its earlier history, both a Neolithic and a Minoan site have so far been identified, the second within the Venetian Castello. The first impression of Khania is that it is an outward-looking place, a cosmopolitan little city. Its inhabitants seem to have a less restricted outlook than many other Cretans, perhaps because Khania was the capital of Crete from 1841 until 1970, throughout the period when the island's final struggle for freedom brought it into wider contact with the outside world.

Appropriately perhaps, since the present-day city was founded by the Venetians in 1252, Khania retains more of the buildings and character of a Venetian city than any other town in Crete. The administrative centre of Venetian Khania (Canea) was the walled citadel known as the Castéllo. Sited on the broad promontory separating the western and eastern basins of the harbour, it was protected on the landward side by a strong wall. Parts of this wall and its towers survive, and built into their structure are many fragments from the Acropolis of the ancient Kydonia which lay on the same site. Within these walls stood the Venetian governor's palace, the cathedral and some private houses belonging to the richer Venetian colonists. Unfortunately, this district was almost entirely destroyed by bombing in 1941, and all that now survives from the Venetian period are such remains as the impressive marble gateway to the Zangaróla mansion and the arcade of the church of St Mark.

At the foot of the Castello, seven stone-vaulted shipsheds survive from an original row of nineteen, built along the southern side of the eastern basin in the last quarter of the sixteenth century. More shipsheds lay on the eastern side of this basin and there were others adjoining the smaller western basin. The harbour is sheltered from the sea by a long rocky wall aligned from west to east and built, together with the lighthouse at its western end, by the Venetians in the fourteenth century (see map). The entrance to both basins lies due north of the western basin which is thus exposed to storms blowing in from the north. The eastern basin is more sheltered, but shallow. In the 1830s the Egyptians built a light shipbuilding yard at the edge of the Venetian breakwater.

Surrounding the two harbour basins and beyond the wall of the Castello were the main residential areas of the Venetian city. Here some districts have retained their Italian character and many of their original Venetian buildings. The streets are narrow, and the houses are tall, massively built of stone and embellished with beautiful ornamental doorways and balconies decorated with ironwork. The Venetian character shows itself most strongly in the Topána quarter, on the west side of the western harbour basin; the many beautifully built Venetian mansions still bear on their façades the coats of arms of their original owners and Latin inscriptions carved in stone. In this district can be seen the Venetian church of San Salvatore (the

THE TOWNS AND URBAN LIFE

Saviour). At the other side of the city, in the south-eastern quarter, the Venetian atmosphere persists in the narrow lanes near the large Venetian church of St Nicholas and the Church of the Áyii Anáryiri. Built in the sixteenth century, this was the only Orthodox church in Venetian Khania and the only public place of Christian worship permitted during the Turkish occupation.

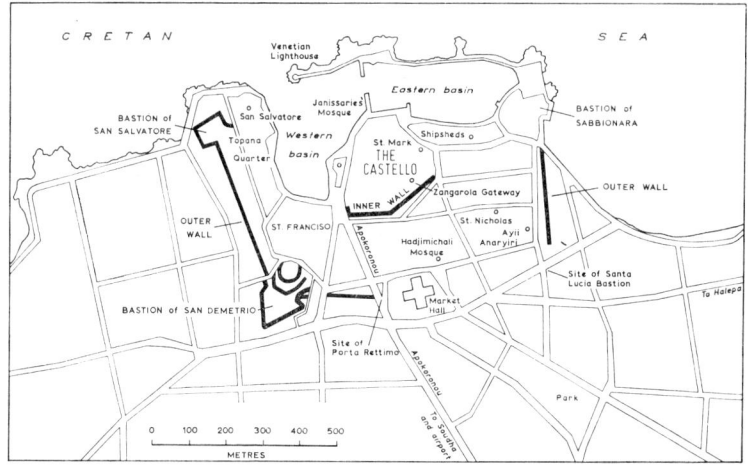

Khania: street plan of the central area

The residential quarters of the Venetian city were protected by a great outer wall, begun at the end of the fifteenth century and completed in 1590. The wall was strengthened by five bastions, two adjacent to the coast at each side of the harbour, and three landward bastions facing south. Of the coast bastions, the north-western San Salvatore is the more striking but has been greatly modified in recent years by the construction upon it of the Xénia Hotel. The north-eastern bastion of Sabbionára or Mocinégo, built after 1549, can still be discerned and an almost intact rampart links it to the partially demolished bastion of Santa Lucía, built 1543–6. The most impressive of

CRETE

the surviving bastions is that of San Dimítrio in the south-west, built 1546–9.

In the centre of the southern stretch of the wall, the main gate, the Pórta Réttimo, was protected by the bastion of Piatatóra—this no longer survives, but has provided the site for the municipal market hall. The only large, covered market in Crete, it was modelled on a similar cruciform building in Marseilles and contains numerous produce shops and stalls. Outside the market to the west, on the site of the Venetian gate, is Apokorónou, the street which still forms the main entrance to Khania. It runs in a straight line from the market square down to the harbour and, according to Spratt, during the period of the Turkish occupation it was lined with bazaars and divided the city into two halves, one Greek and one Turkish.

The Turks took Khania in 1645, after a siege lasting fifty-five days. Numerous Turkish houses were built within the walled town and most of the Venetian churches were converted into mosques. The Venetian church of St Nicholas Splanzias, known by the Turks as the Imperial Mosque, still retains its minaret, as does the Hadjimicháli Mosque near the market hall. The largest and best preserved Venetian church in Crete, the church of St Francis, was converted into a mosque to commemorate Youssouf Pasha, who first took the city for the Turks; in its enclosure can be seen a beautiful Turkish fountain. Down by the harbour the Janissaries' own small mosque still stands.

During most of their occupation, the Turks would not permit the construction of houses outside the walls. Some distance away to the east there was in the nineteenth century a separate Arab village of 2–3,000 people. Once extra-mural development was permitted, a new small town, in European style, grew up to contrast sharply with the old. No longer small, it has spread over a wide area. The numerous suburbs include Halépa in the east which became an important administrative district during the occupation by the Great Powers.

Khania's principal functions have long been those of adminis-

THE TOWNS AND URBAN LIFE

tration and commerce. It serves an extensive and rich agricultural hinterland, including all western Crete and the Apokorona to the east. Its own industries are small and based mainly upon local agricultural raw materials: olive oil and soap works, tanneries, small foundries, wine-making cooperatives, and industries related to the citrus fruit production of the surrounding coastal areas.

The port functions of Khania have been transferred from the small and inadequate Venetian harbour to the nearby deep-water port of Soudha, which has direct modern car-ferry links with Piraeus and facilities for receiving grain and other imports. Adjacent to the port is a large flour mill. On the opposite side of Soudha Bay, near the village of Stérnes, is Khania airport with domestic flights to Athens and other Greek cities.

The city of Khania, although closely rivalling Iraklion in size, has a more relaxed and tranquil atmosphere. Its climate is milder and more agreeable, and the abundance of trees in and around the city greatly adds to its attractiveness. Observed from a café table beside the Venetian harbour, or from the broad avenues flanked by large ornate villas and ornamental gardens in the older parts of the 'new town', Khania is a city with a strong historical presence and one that is made even more attractive by the warmth and friendliness of its inhabitants.

RETHYMNON

In the days when the internal trade of Crete was carried by coastal shipping rather than by road, Rethymnon became important as a collecting centre for olive oil from the coastal plain and for cheese and wine from the hills farther inland. With the development of the road from Iraklion to Khania, these activities grew and were supplemented by soap-making and by a small growth of service industries. Rethymnon is the third largest town in Crete. Plans for its development, both before and after World War II, included proposals for improving the harbour, and impressive moles now protect a large area.

CRETE

The new harbour was rendered useless by silting almost as soon as it was finished, and attempts to clear it have not been successful. Shipping is restricted to such fishing and coastal craft as can use the old Venetian harbour. The spectacular development of road transport during the last decade and the opening of the National Road along the north coast have more than compensated for the disappearance of sea-borne traffic. Under the development plan a modern cheese-factory has been built; this produces a large part of the speciality cheeses of Crete, of which the best-known is *graviéra*, a hard cheese of the Gruyère type.

The name of Rethymnon (called Rithymna by Ptolemy) derives from the ancient Greek *reithron*, meaning a stream of water. The promontory on which the great Venetian fortress stands was occupied in classical antiquity. In medieval times the town seems to have been without walls until it was fortified by the first Venetian colonists at the beginning of the thirteenth century. The walls then built protected the settlement on the landward side alone. It was not until the middle of the sixteenth century that the threat of invasion by the Turks and the reality of attacks by pirates led to the building of a fort on the promontory. The foundation stone of the Fortézza was laid on 13 September 1573. Disputes about forced labour, bribery of the contractors by the Greeks to avoid having to work, and continued appeals to Venice delayed the work, so that the circuit of the walls was not completed until 1578, and the earth filling not for another five years.

The question then arose as to whether the inhabitants of the town should all be moved into the fortress, alongside the Venetian administration. The argument was settled in 1645 by the Turkish attack on Rethymnon. The lower town was soon over-run and, on 11 October, both Greeks and Venetians took refuge in the fortress. During the siege the Turks fired leaflets into the fortress calling on the Cretans among the defenders to lay down their arms and not to fight for their Venetian oppressors. The decision to abandon Rethymnon had already been

THE TOWNS AND URBAN LIFE

taken in Venice and, on 20 October, a galley of the Republic put into the harbour; some mercenaries were disembarked and the ship took on board the Venetian Rector and his staff. Thereupon, says a modern Greek historian, 'the blood froze in the defenders' veins'. The fortress capitulated on 4 November, and 1,500 of the inhabitants were evacuated to Corfu, Zakynthos and others of the Ionian Islands then in Venetian hands. The Fortezza was at once taken over by the Turks, and history heard no more of Rethymnon until 16 December 1898, when the flag of independence was broken out over the walls of that same fortress which had been for so many years the visible symbol of slavery and of oppression by a foreign tyrant.

Rethymnon is the only town in Crete which is not approached by a main road leading to and through its centre. Arriving by road, the visitor finds himself in a broad boulevard running along the southern edge of the town. It requires a positive decision to make a diversion down one of the narrow streets leading to the sea-front, and only thus can one approach the central part of the town. Rethymnon today has no obvious town centre. The streets of the old town are flanked by tall shuttered houses, many of them Turkish, with corbelled upper storeys, iron-barred windows and projecting balconies. Ancient alleyways sometimes give a view of a slender minaret rising above the squat domes of its mosque. Many Venetian buildings, including a tower carrying a sundial, have been pulled down, but the Loggia and several sixteenth- and seventeenth-century doorways remain. In character and atmosphere the town is inward-looking, rejecting both the past, symbolised by the deserted waterfront and the battle-scarred Fortezza, and the future, which lies in claiming a share of the wealth now passing along the great highway.

AYIOS NIKOLAOS

The earliest British Admiralty chart of eastern Crete, engraved

CRETE

in 1858, does not show the town of Ayios Nikolaos. Captain Spratt, from whose original survey the chart was produced, visited the district and described the offshore island of 'Nikolo' and, on the main island close to the sea, a curious lake which was almost circular and said by local people to be bottomless. With a characteristic blend of scientific curiosity and practical seamanship, Captain Spratt took soundings in the lake and found its depth in the centre to be 64 metres (210ft).

Some years later, in 1869, the Turkish governor of Lassithi, Kostis Adhosidhis Pasha, encouraged settlers to found a new town adjacent to the lake where there was already a hamlet. The lake was turned into a small harbour by the construction of a canal some 5 metres (16ft) wide and 1 metre (3ft) deep, linking it to the sea. Thus the Pasha founded a town which was later to take over the role of regional capital from his own chosen capital of Neapolis. The new town of Ayios Nikolaos grew and an outer harbour was built, to which there has recently been added a long jetty, so that the port can now accommodate medium-sized coasting vessels.

The old lake, formerly known as Mandraki (Little Sheepfold) and now called Voulisméni, is accessible only to small dinghies, and part of it is sometimes used as an open-air swimming pool. Backed by a spectacular cliff, Voulismeni forms an attractive focus for the town grouped around it. The two parallel main streets lie just to the south of the lake and ascend the hill from the harbour to the main Venizélos Square. Other streets at right-angles lead southwards to the Nomarchía—the administrative offices of the Nomos—sited here since 1904, and to the town's main beach. The basic plan, like that of other towns of the same period, such as Neapolis and Sitia, is roughly a grid-iron.

Although the present town of Ayios Nikolaos is modern in design and construction, its site is ancient. The tourist, staying at one of Ayios Nikolaos' many excellent new hotels, can visit the spectacularly sited ruins of Láto, high on its ridge to the south-west. Three thousand years ago, Lato was the principal

THE TOWNS AND URBAN LIFE

city in this part of Crete, and had as its port a subsidiary settlement known as Láto pros Kamára, on the site of the modern Ayios Nikolaos.

At the end of the twelfth century the Genoese erected a castle on the hill south of the lake; this strongpoint later passed through Venetian and Turkish hands before being destroyed by the Turks in 1645. Under the Venetians, the town's primary function was that of a commercial port. For their main naval and military base in eastern Crete, the Venetians developed the nearby islet of Spinalonga, off the northern tip of the Spinalonga peninsula. Such was the strength of this position that the Venetians held Spinalonga Island until 1715, long after they had lost the rest of Crete to the Turks.

After its evacuation by the Turks in 1904, Spinalonga Island became the site of Crete's last leper colony. In earlier times there had been several leper villages. Captain Spratt describes the piteous condition of the lepers as they begged outside the eastern Lazaretto Gate of Iraklion; there was another leper village, for the Eparchy of Sitia, about $1\frac{1}{2}$ kilometres north of Ierapetra. The leper colony of Spinalonga, deserted for some years, had a population of 277 in 1931.

This part of Crete, in the vicinity of Ayios Nikolaos, has seen many curious developments throughout its history. The ancient city of Oloüs once flourished on the southern part of the peninsula, adjacent to the isthmus; its ruins lie submerged beneath shallow water. The great Bay of Elounda, sheltered by the peninsula, was used between the wars as an airbase for the giant flying boats of Imperial Airways.

The Spinalonga peninsula, the ancient cities of Lato, Olous and Gournia, the modern towns of Neapolis, Kritsa and Ierapetra, and the spectacular mountain plateau of Lassithi all lie within a short distance of Ayios Nikolaos. The town itself hibernates peacefully in winter, but for many years now—since the 'good old days' when it had its own direct air service—it has been enlivened throughout the spring and summer months by visitors from many countries. The intrinsic charm of the town and its citizens, and the convenience of its situation, draw many people back to it year after year.

SITIA

The town of Sitia is small, peaceful and remote. It has long been the eastern terminus of the main west-east road, but has only recently become readily accessible with the completion of the Kavousi–Sitia stretch of the National Road. This road climbs across the slopes of Kavousi Effendi, high above the spectacular cliffs of the northern coast, and leads straight into the town of Sitia, sited on a hillside at the western edge of a large sandy bay, near the mouth of the River Pantelis. There is a small harbour, backed by a picturesque array of lime-washed houses, cafés and small restaurants. From the waterfront, short narrow streets lead up the steep hillsides; other, longer streets run at right angles to these, thus forming the grid-iron plan of the Turkish town laid out in 1870.

Under its ancient name of Eteia, Sitia served as the harbour of Praissós and later grew as a city in its own right. The town was destroyed by earthquakes in 1303 and 1508, and by the pirate Barbarossa in 1538. Anticipating that they would not be able to hold it against the Turks, the Venetians destroyed both the town and the fortress in 1651. The ruins of their fort can still be seen on the hillside at the northern edge of the town. Destroyed and abandoned, Sitia remained virtually uninhabited under the Turks until the present town was laid out in 1870.

The economic development of Sitia, which had lagged noticeably behind that of towns farther to the west, has been accelerated recently by the completion of the National Road and the construction of an irrigation system in that part of the valley of the River Pantelis immediately south of the town. Before irrigation, the summer view of Sitia was of a small town by the sea, at the mouth of a river that was often dry, and backed by a parched hinterland, except for a narrow green strip in the centre of the valley. Following the exploitation of ground-

THE TOWNS AND URBAN LIFE

water resources underlying the valley floor, the narrow strip has broadened out into a wide band of green crossing the valley and extending part-way up the adjacent hillsides.

Sultanas are the chief product of the irrigated area, but other cash crops such as table grapes and early vegetables are gradually increasing in importance. The markets of the west have been opened up and the new road has also encouraged more tourists to visit Sitia and use it as a base for exploring the far eastern end of the island. Hotels are being built, there is a good sandy beach adjacent to the town, and within reach are the Minoan sites of Praissos, Palaikastro and Zakros, the fortified monastery of Toplou and the palm beach of Vai.

Morosini Fountain, Iraklion

11 SERVICES AND ADMINISTRATION

HOTELS

SINCE the early 1960s there has been a spate of hotel building in Crete centred in and around Iraklion, Khania and Ayios Nikolaos and, to a lesser extent, Rethymnon and Sitia. These towns now offer a comprehensive range of purpose-built, modern hotels varying from the simple and functional to the lavish and luxurious. All hotels in Crete, as throughout Greece, are officially inspected and classified according to the standard of accommodation they offer. The luxury category are free to charge what prices they like, but all other hotels are required by law to keep them within certain fixed limits as defined for each category, being higher for the 'A' class than the 'B', lower in the 'C' or 'Γ' category, and so on. Prices of meals and of drinks served in the hotel bar are also regulated, although alcoholic drinks are usually much cheaper obtained outside the hotel. Within the hotels, bar prices must be on display, and each hotel room must have a card showing the approved room rate, seasonal price variations and details of special services and facilities. The standard room in a modern hotel has two single beds, its own bathroom and toilet and, usually, a small private balcony. Nearly all hotels include a version of the Continental breakfast in the room price, and half and full board terms are often available in the larger hotels. Where the hotel does have a restaurant, there is usually a choice of Greek and European menus. The quality of hotel food, like that of Cretan restaurants in general, varies enormously and the visitor who strikes unlucky the first time should not be discouraged.

SERVICES AND ADMINISTRATION

If large hotels complete with restaurants, television lounges and private swimming pools have little attraction, there are many small *pensions* in the old Turkish quarters of the towns, tucked away in narrow back streets. These offer adequate but inexpensive rooms, usually with shared bathroom and toilet facilities. Many private households are also willing to let rooms and addresses may be obtained from the local tourist police (see p 192).

Many of the new hotels have been built on redeveloped sites in the city centres, close to banks, restaurants, bus stops, museums and historic monuments; others are sited to provide access to other amenities, such as sand and sea. Many of these hotels, located several kilometres from the main towns, have their own private beaches and offer a full range of facilities; some provide daily transport to the nearest town. A few of the largest, such as one on the outskirts of Iraklion and another just west of Ayios Nikolaos, resemble miniature new towns, with small private bungalows clustered round a central social and amenity complex offering, at a price, bars, restaurants and lounges.

Fortunately, most of these developments have been carefully landscaped and attractively designed with the result that, thus far, Crete has not suffered some of the worst visual side effects of a growing tourist industry.

POSTS AND TELECOMMUNICATIONS

Post services in Crete are operated by the Greek Post Office. Internally, the postal network extends to every village and hamlet; there are at least daily services between the principal towns, and up to four urban deliveries per day, Sundays included. A parcel post is also operated. The postal arrangements in Crete, as in mainland Greece, compare very favourably with those in other European countries. Air mail is carried on almost every aircraft between Athens and Iraklion and Khania, and on direct scheduled flights abroad.

CRETE

All domestic and foreign telephone and telegraph operations are conducted by the Greek Telecommunications Organisation (OTE). Inter-city dialling is available from all urban private telephones to all towns in Crete and to most of the Greek mainland. There are public call-boxes at the OTE offices, where local calls may be dialled, but all other calls are connected only on written application to the counter clerk. As soon as the call is connected, the caller is directed by the clerk to one of the boxes reserved for long-distance calls. This may seem a cumbrous procedure, but in practice it works smoothly and quickly and meets the needs of those users as yet unfamiliar with sophisticated equipment. In some remote places there are no private telephone subscribers, and in these the OTE maintains an office with a telephone available for official and private use. These village offices are not on line all the time, but calls may be booked for those times when the lines are open. The telegraph service is popular, being both rapid and comparatively cheap for internal messages. The international Telex service is available to private subscribers, and Telex messages may also be sent by the public to Telex subscribers through the OTE offices and at a cheaper rate than ordinary telegrams.

THE CHURCH

The Church in Crete is part of the Greek Orthodox Church, under the jurisdiction of the Patriarch of Athens who, in turn, is subject to the rule of the Ecumenical Patriarch at Constantinople. The senior prelate in Crete is the Archbishop of Iraklion, whose cathedral church is St Titus in Iraklion. Under him, control of the Church is exercised by the Metropolitan bishops. The monasteries are for the most part autonomous in their temporal affairs, but are spiritually subject either to the local Metropolitan or to the monastery which founded them.

SERVICES AND ADMINISTRATION

CIVIL ADMINISTRATION

Crete is divided into four large administrative divisions, known as Nomoi, each of which roughly corresponds in size and function to an English county. The Nomoi of Khania and Rethymnon in the west and Iraklion in the centre have as their capitals the cities of the same name; in the east, the capital of the Nomos of Lassithi is Ayios Nikolaos. Below the Nomoi in the hierarchy of local government are the rural districts (Eparchies), the city and town authorities (Démoi) and the rural communes (Koinótites) (see Table 6). These are the channels through which the political power, centred in Athens, is deployed.

The ministries of the central government have regional offices in Crete, as in every other administrative and planning region of Greece. These offices are situated in Iraklion, the administrative capital of the island. Chief among them are the Ministry of Co-ordination, responsible for development planning, and the Ministry of Agriculture which has an Inspectorate-General of Agriculture and also controls the Land Reclamation Service. The Departments of Trade, Industry and Economics, and the Mercantile Marine are similarly represented.

Table 6

ADMINISTRATIVE DIVISIONS (30 JUNE 1972)

Nomos	Eparchies	Demoi	Communes
Iraklion	7	3	191
Khania	5	2	162
Lassithi	4	4	88
Rethymnon	4	2	131
All Crete	*20*	*11*	*572*

ADMINISTRATION OF THE LAW

Law in Greece is codified in both the civil and criminal branches, so that there is no body of case law, and the courts are guided in their decisions by existing laws and decrees. Minor offences are tried by summary courts sitting in the towns and presided over by a local magistrate. More serious crimes and substantial civil cases are remitted to a higher court, and appeals against the decisions of this and of the summary courts are heard by courts of appeal, of which the highest is the Supreme Court in Athens.

Public order and law enforcement

The maintenance of public order and the enforcement of the law is the responsibility of the police (*Khorophylaki*), who carry out all police functions in the towns and villages and in the countryside. A specially trained and equipped branch, the traffic police (*Trohaia*), deals with traffic control, motoring offences and road accidents. Road discipline, including speed limits and parking restrictions, is strictly enforced. Officers of this branch may be recognised by their shoulder flashes. Constables in the ordinary uniformed branch of the police wear two white chevrons edged with black on their sleeves. Warrant officers and commissioned ranks wear badges similar to those of corresponding rank in the army.

Tourist police

In centres of tourism there is usually a section of the tourist police (*Touristikí Astynomía*) with an office of its own where inquiries may be made. The officers of this branch wear distinctive shoulder flashes and their function is to assist tourists, both Greek and foreign. Their offices keep lists of local accommodation for visitors and will assist in making a fair deal with the landlord. They are not able to intervene directly in cases of overcharging in shops or restaurants, since these are under the control of the market police section of the general police force.

Other officials

In the villages and the countryside the field guards (*Agrophýlakes*) walk or ride round the fields, vineyards, orchards and

SERVICES AND ADMINISTRATION

gardens keeping a look out for pilfering of crops and for stray animals causing damage.

At all seaports, control of the arrivals and departures of vessels is exercised by officers and ratings of the Harbour Corps (*Limenikón Sóma*), who wear naval uniform with the distinguishing mark of their corps. They control movement within the port waters and police the port area.

EDUCATION

Education in Greece is organised on three levels: primary, secondary and higher. The school year begins in October and ends in June. Education is provided free of charge in all state schools and is compulsory at the primary level. Nursery schools are available for children of at least three and a half years of age. Primary school (*Demotikón*) education starts at five and a half years, when children are enrolled for a full six-year course. Those children who cannot attend school during the day are allowed to attend night-schools, of which there are eleven in Crete.

Table 7

SCHOOLS (1971)

Nomos	Nursery Schools	Primary Schools	Gymnasia
Iraklion	48	307	25
Khania	31	224	15
Lassithi	23	113	8
Rethymnon	15	166	8
All Crete	*117*	*810*	*56*

Secondary education is provided at the Gymnasium; it comprises a six-grade course divided into higher and lower levels. All children who have successfully completed their primary education can enrol at their local Gymnasium, provided that they pass the entrance examinations. On the successful completion of the course, students receive a certificate of secondary education. Admission to centres of higher education usually depends upon the possession of this certificate and upon successfully completing the entrance examinations, although the exact regulations vary from place to place.

In addition to the four principal universities, all in mainland Greece, there are vocational and technical schools at various levels; in Crete, these include the Khania Higher School of Home Economics and a large new technical college at Neapolis.

The visitor to Crete will be struck by the large number of language schools which flourish in the towns. These are privately owned or, in a few cases, sponsored by the propaganda services of a foreign nation. Many of the owners are Greek women and the teachers, all of whom must be qualified, are mostly European or American. The standard of teaching is generally high, and in some schools electronic teaching aids are used.

HOSPITALS AND MEDICAL SERVICES

Crete has sixty-seven hospitals with a total, in 1971, of 2,452 beds; these include eight public hospitals with 1,045 beds and fifty-nine private clinics with 1,407 beds. In addition to the large general hospitals, such as that at Iraklion, there are many smaller clinics specialising in obstetrics and gynaecology, pediatrics and neuro-psychiatry. The doctors and dentists are mostly based in the main towns of the north coast; the Nomoi of Lassithi and Rethymnon are generally less well provided with facilities and expertise than are Iraklion and Khania.

Table 8

HEALTH SERVICES (1971)

Nomos	Hospitals and clinics	Number of beds	Doctors	Dentists
Iraklion	33	1,049	186	46
Khania	20	914	143	27
Lassithi	4	248	46	13
Rethymnon	10	241	43	12
All Crete	67	2,452	418	98

APPENDIX

THE OFFSHORE ISLANDS

ONLY one of the islets off the shores of Crete is inhabited. They have little or no timber cover, and are generally barren and waterless. In the list given here, the name of each island has been translated, where a known meaning exists.

North coast—from west to east

Pontikonísi	Mouse Island
Grabóusa Island	Sometimes called Ímeri Grabóusa: Tame Grabousa
Ágria Grabóusa	Wild Grabousa
Áyii Theódori	In the Gulf of Khania; this island is maintained as a sanctuary for the *agrimi* or *Ibex creticus*, threatened with extinction in its natural habitat in the White Mountains
Soúdha Island	The fortress island guarding Soudha Bay
Dhía Island	The Bright or Shining Island, sometimes called Stándia from εἰς τὰν Δία as Stamboul from εἰς τὰν πόλιν. About 265 metres (869ft) high in the centre, it is covered with low scrub. A small rabbit with a long name (*Oryctolagus cuniculus huxlei*) is found on Dhia, but not on Crete, where the light-coloured hare (*Lepus creticus*) occurs. An attempt to introduce the *agrimi* to Dhia was unsuccessful because of the presence of goats, which diluted the stock of the ibex
Spinalónga Island	Long Thorn Island; at the entrance to Spinalonga or Póros Bay. Once a Venetian fortress, it was held for some time by Venice after the adjacent mainland had fallen to the

CRETE

	Turks. In 1903 it became a leper colony, and remained so for about fifty years. Spinalonga peninsula, cut off from Crete by the manmade passage leading to the salterns in Poros Bay, is technically an island
Kolokýthia Islet	Little Marrow (Squash) Island; off the east coast of Spinalonga peninsula
Mikró Nisí	Little Island; 23 metres (75ft) high, off Ayios Nikolaos to the north
Ayios Nikolaos Island	Off Ayios Nikolaos; 45 metres (148ft) high. An attempt to keep *Ibex creticus* here was unsuccessful
Konída Island	In the Gulf of Mirabello, off Pakhía Ámmos
Pseíra Island	Louse Island; so-called from its shape and colour; 2½ kilometres long, 230 metres (755ft) high. Now barren and uninhabited, it contains the remains of a Minoan city which flourished in the EM II period; it was excavated by Seager in 1912
Mókhlos Island	Only 150 metres (492ft) from Crete, to which it was joined by a causeway in Minoan times; the site of a prosperous EM II city
The Dhionisiádhis Islands	This group consists of Paximádhi (Dry Biscuit), the most northern and the smallest; Dragonádha, the largest; and Gianisádha

South coast—from west to east

Elaphónisos	Deer Island; a narrow, flat islet very close to the mainland. A juniper (*Juniperus macrocarpa*) is found on the sandy shores growing sometimes to a height of 5 metres (16ft)
Low Islet	Named on Admiralty Chart; about 800 metres (½ mile) off Elaphónisos
Gavdhópoula	The Chick of Gávdhos. A limestone islet about 3 kilometres long from north-west to south-east, and 800 metres (½ mile) wide. The coast is steep, and the land rises to about 150 metres (492ft). It lies 5 kilometres to the north-west of Gavdhos
Gávdhos	Formerly called Clauda; 37 kilometres south of Khóra Sphakión. The only inhabited offshore island—population 142 in 1971—its

APPENDIX

	area is about 37 square kilometres; the heights in the centre rise to over 300 metres (984ft). The south-west coast consists of steep limestone cliffs with no inlets. The other coasts are lower and less precipitous; there is a small harbour south-east of Cape Sarakinikó. The interior is cultivated and the main settlements—Kastrí, Ámbelos, Xenianá and Vatsianá—all stand above 200 metres (656ft). The lower parts of the island are covered with garrigue and there are a few low pine trees and junipers. Three settlements—Áyios Geórgios, Sarakinikó and Panagóula—have been abandoned for lack of water
Paximádhia Islands	Dry Biscuit Islands; situated almost centrally in the Gulf of Messara
Gaidhourónisi	Donkey Island; off Ierápetra. Also called Khrisí (the Golden). On the sandy beaches the juniper (*J. macrocarpa*) flourishes
Kouphónisi	Light Island (in weight)

East coast—from north to south

Élasa Island	A grey limestone island with a flat top more than 100 metres (328ft) above the sea; 2½ kilometres off the peninsula of Toplóu
Grándes Islands	An island about 1½ kilometres long and 40 metres (131ft) high, and two small islets; in Grándes Bay to the north-west of Cape Pláka

BIBLIOGRAPHY

ADMIRALTY. *Mediterranean Pilot, vol 4 . . . including also the Island of Crete* (7th ed 1941)
ADMIRALTY, NAVAL INTELLIGENCE DIVISION. *Greece*, Geographical Handbook Ser BR 516, 516A, 516B (1944–5)
AGRIDEV LTD. *Crete: Development plan 1965–1975* (Tel-Aviv, 1965)
ALLBAUGH, L. G. *Crete: A Case Study of an Underdeveloped Area* (Princeton, NJ, 1953)
ANNA COMNENA, PRINCESS (early 12th c AD). *The Alexiad of Anna Comnena*, trans from the Greek by E. R. A. Sewter (Harmondsworth, Middx, 1969)
APPIAN (2nd c AD). *Appian's Roman History, with an English translation by H. White*, vol 1, book 5: Of Sicily and the other islands, part 6, in Greek and English (1912)
BATTYE, A. B. R. T. *Camping in Crete, with Notes upon the Animal and Plant Life of the Island* (1913)
BOURNE, K. 'Great Britain and the Cretan Revolt, 1866–1869', *Slavonic Review*, 35 (1956), 74–94
BOWMAN, J. *Crete*, traveller's guide (rev ed 1969)
BRAIDER, D. *The Master Painter: A Novel Based on the Life of El Greco* (1968)
BRAUDEL, F. *The Mediterranean*, trans from the French (1972)
BURGEL, G. *Pobia: étude géographique d'un village crétois* (Athens, 1965)
CHADWICK, J. *The decipherment of Linear B* (Harmondsworth, Middx, 1961)
CHAPOUTHIER, F. and CHARBONNEAUX, J. 'Fouilles exécutées à Mallia; premier rapport, 1922–24', *Ecole Française d'Athènes, Etudes Crétoises*, 1 (1928). (Further reports in later vols of series)
CORNARO, F. *Creta Sacra* (Venice, 1755)
DAVIDSON, A. *Mediterranean seafood* (Harmondsworth, Middx, 1972)
ELLIADI, N. *Crete, Past and Present* (1933)
EVANS, Sir A. J. *The Palace of Minos*, 5 vols (1921–36)
FAURE, P. 'Fonctions des cavernes crétoises', *Ecole Française d'Athènes, Travaux et Memoires*, Fasc. 14 (1965)

BIBLIOGRAPHY

FIELDING, X. *The Stronghold* (1953)
FOREIGN OFFICE. *Eastern Papers*, Part 5 (122 of 1854) (1854)
GEOPONICA (7th or 10th C AD). *Geoponica. Agricultural pursuits*, trans from the Greek by T. Owen; 2 vols (1805-6)
GERLAND, E. 'Histoire de la noblesse Crétoise au Moyen Age', *Revue de l'Orient Latin*, 10 and 11 (1907)
GEROLA, G. *Monumenti veneti nell' isola di Creta* (Venice, 1906-32)
GREGOROVIUS, F. *Geschichte der Stadt Athen* (Stuttgart, 1889)
HOMER (c 1000 BC). *Iliad* and *Odyssey*, trans from the Greek by E. V. Rieu (Harmondsworth, Middx, 1969, 1970)
HOOD, M. S. F. *The Minoans: Crete in the Bronze Age* (1971)
HOWARD, Sir E. *Theatre of Life—Seen from the Pit, 1863-1905* (1935)
HURST, L. H. 'The Mountains of Crete', *Alpine Journal*, 65 (1960), 208-13
HUTCHINSON, R. W. *Prehistoric Crete*, rev ed (Harmondsworth, Middx, 1968)
JEFFREY, L. H. *The Local Scripts of Archaic Greece* (Oxford, 1961)
KAZANTZAKIS, N. *Freedom and Death*, trans from the Greek (1956)
——. *Zorba the Greek*, trans from the Greek (1952)
KOBER, A. E. 'The Minoan Scripts: Fact and Theory', *American Journal of Archaeology*, 52 (1948), 82-103
KOLODNY, E-Y. 'Constitution et évolution démographique d'un isolat en montagne; le bassin du Lassithi en Crète', *Revue de Géographie de Lyon*, 44 (1969), 193-225
KOSSERIS, C. and CLUTTON, E. 'A Review of the Development Plan for Crete, 1965-75', *Geographical Journal*, 134 (1968), 64-9
MAKRIDAKIS, A. H. *The Tourist's Guide for the City of Khania* (Khania, undated late 1960s)
MARINATOS, S. 'The Volcanic Destruction of Minoan Crete', *Antiquity*, 13 (1939), 425-39
—— ed. *Acta of the International Scientific Congress on the Volcano of Thera, 1969* (Athens, 1971)
MARRIOTT, Sir A. J. *The Eastern Question*, 4th ed (Oxford, 1940)
MILLER, W. *Essays on the Latin Orient* (Cambridge, 1921)
——. *The Ottoman empire and its successors, 1801-1927, with an appendix, 1927-1936* (Cambridge, 1936)
MORGAN, G. 'English State Papers on the Siege of Candia', *Cretica Chronica*, 13 (1959)
Moss, W. S. *Ill Met by Moonlight* (1950)
NATIONAL STATISTICAL SERVICE OF GREECE. *Agricultural statistics of Greece year 1966*. In Greek and English (Athens, 1968)
——. *Population of Greece at the Census of 14 March 1971*. In Greek and English (Athens, 1972)

CRETE

———. *Statistical Yearbook 1972*. In Greek and English (Athens, 1973)

NOIRET, H. ed. *Documents inédits pour servir à l'histoire de la domination vénitienne en Crète de 1380 à 1485* (Paris, 1892)

OSTROGORSKY, G. *History of the Byzantine State*, trans from the German (Oxford, 1956)

PALMER, L. R. *Myceneans and Minoans*, 2nd ed (1965)

PASHLEY, R. *Travels in Crete* (Cambridge, 1837)

PATON, D. 'Flower hunting in Crete', *Geographical Magazine*, 39 (1967), 378–86

PAUSANIAS (2nd c AD). *Guide to Greece*, trans from the Greek by P. Levi (Harmondsworth, Middx, 1971)

PECHOUX, P-Y. 'La polje de Lassithi (Crète orientale)', *Revue de Géographie de Lyon*, 43 (1968), 395–414

PENDLEBURY, J. D. S. *The Archaeology of Crete* (1939)

———. *A Handbook to the Palace of Minos, Knossos* (1954)

PEUTINGER TABLE (AD 1265). *Tabula peutingeriana; die Peutingerische Tafel*, ed K. Miller (Stuttgart, 1962), 13th c copy of Roman map

PINDAR (518–438 BC). *Odes*, trans from the Greek by C. M. Bowra (Harmondsworth, Middx, 1969)

POLUNIN, O. and HUXLEY, A. J. *Flowers of the Mediterranean* (1965)

PREVELAKIS, P. *Chronique d'une cité*, trans from the Greek (Paris, 1960)

———. *Le Crétois*, trans from the Greek (Paris, 1962)

PROCEEDINGS, SECOND INTERNATIONAL CRETOLOGICAL CONGRESS, 1966. (Athens, 1968), 3 vol multilingual collection of papers, mainly on history of Crete

PSYCHOUDAKIS, G. *The Cretan Runner*, trans from the Greek (1955)

PTOLEMY (2nd c AD). *Geographia*, with an introduction by R. A. Skelton (Amsterdam, 1966)

RAPP, G., COOKE, S. R. B. and HENRICKSON, E. 'Pumice from Thera (Santorini) Identified from a Greek Mainland Expedition', *Science*, 179 (1973), 471–3

RAULIN, F. V. *Description physique et naturelle de l'isle de Crète* (Paris, 1869)

ROBERTS, D. F. 'The Cretans: a Geographical Analysis of some Aspects of their Physical Anthropology', *Journal of the Royal Anthropological Institute*, 84 (1954), 145–57

ROBERTSON, J. and GARDINER, D. *Twelve days in Crete* (1972)

SETTON, K. M. *Catalan Domination of Athens, 1311–1388* (Cambridge, Mass, 1948)

SIMPSON, H. C. C. D. 'With the International Field Force in Crete, 1897', *Proceedings of the Royal Artillery Institute*, 26 (1899), 519–39

SKINNER, J. E. H. *Roughing it in Crete in 1867* (1868)

SMITH, M. L. *The Great Island: a Study of Crete* (1965)

BIBLIOGRAPHY

SPANAKIS, S. *Crete*, vol 1, trans from the Greek (Iraklion, 1964); vol 2, in Greek (Iraklion, undated late 1960s)
SPRATT, T. A. B. *Travels and Researches in Crete* (1865)
STADIASMUS (AD 550) published in: Mueller, G. *Geographici Graeci Minores*, 2 vols (Paris, 1855–61). The Stadiasmus is a 6th c equivalent of the Admiralty's *Mediterranean Pilot*
STEWART, I. M. G. *The Struggle for Crete 20th May–1st June 1941* (1966)
STILLMAN, W. J. *American Consul in a Cretan War* (Austin, Tex, 1966), rev ed of *The Cretan Insurrection of 1866-7-8* (New York, 1874)
STRABO (1st c BC). *The Geography of Strabo*, trans from the Greek by H. L. Jones, 8 vols (1917–32)
TEDDER, A. W. *With Prejudice: the War Memoirs of Marshal of the Royal Air Force Lord Tedder* (1966)
VENTRIS, M. 'A Note on Decipherment Methods', *Antiquity*, 27 (1953), 200–6
VENTRIS, M. and CHADWICK, J. 'Evidence for Greek Dialect in the Mycenaean Archives', *Journal of Hellenic Studies*, 73 (1953), 84–103
WAVELL, General Sir A. 'Middle East Dispatches, 1941', *London Gazette*, 37609, 37638 (1946)
WILLETTS, R. F. *Everyday Life in Ancient Crete* (1969)
—— ed and trans. *The Law Code of Gortyn* (Berlin, 1967)
XANTHOUDIDIS, S. A. *Handax–Iraklion*. In Greek (Iraklion, 1964)
——. *The Vaulted Tombs of Messara*, trans from the Greek (Liverpool, 1924)
——. *The Venetian Domination in Crete and the struggle of the Cretans against the Venetians* (Athens, 1939), special supplement to *Byzantinisch-Neugriechischen Jahrbüchern*, no 34
YIOUMBAKIS, M. G. *Fortezza: the history of the Venetian fortress of Rethymnon*. In Greek (Rethymnon, 1970)
ZAMBELIOS, S. *A Cretan marriage*. In Greek (Turin, 1871)
ZOHARY, M. and ORSHAN, G. *An Outline of the Geobotany of Crete* (Jerusalem, 1966). Special supplement to *Israel Journal of Botany*, vol 14

INDEX

Administration, 96, 97, 101-4, 133, 141, 166-8, 180-1, 184, 191-3
Agate, 78, 79
Agave, 47
Agriculture, 23, 26, 28, 39, 45-55 *passim*, 75, 105-6, 146-53
Air transport, 13, 17-18
Akrotiri, 17, 22, 160
Almyros, 30, 113
Amnissos, 31, 171
Anapodharis, R., 32
Anatolia, 68, 72, 74, 80
Angeliana, 24
Anhydrite, 40
Ano Moulia, 31
Ano Viannos, 32
Anoyia, 28, 29, 43-5, 144, 166
Antikythera, 14, 16
Arabs, 93, 94-6, 169, 174, 180
Archaeology, 67-91 *passim*, 94, 184-5, 187
Architecture, 72, 74, 78, 86, 144-5, 169-89 *passim*
Arkadhi, 129-30
Arkalokhori, 32, 53, 166
Arkhanes, 30, 166
Asia Minor, 72, 74, 75, 135
Askiphos, 26
Asphodel, 48
Asterousian Mts, 31, 32-5
Athens, 13, 17, 18, 181
Avdhou, 35
Ayia Galini, 28, 35

Ayia Roumeli, 25, 60
Ayia Triadha, 75-6, 86
Ayia Varvara, 29
Ayii Dheka, 31, 32
Ayii Theodori, 195
Ayios Nikolaos, 16, 37-8, 56-7, 63, 64, 66, 101, 165, 167, 183-6, 188, 189, 191

Beaches, 21, 25, 28, 35, 39, 40, 184, 187, 189
Bronze, 78
Buses, 15-16, 62-6 *passim*, 168
Byzantine Empire, 94-9 *passim*

Caïques, 14, 56, 61
Carob, 47, 49, 152
Caves: 72, 170; Dhikti, 36; Idha, 29, 64; Matala, 35
Cereals, 26, 48, 53-4, 105, 149, 152
Charcoal, 162-3
Cheese, 23, 138, 154, 182
Chios, 53
Churches, 25, 37, 95, 96, 173-4, 178-80 *passim*
Cinemas, 43, 168, 171
Climate, 41-5, 76, 181
Coasts, 45-8; east, 39; north, 21-3, 30-1, 40, 59, 61, 62, 64, 167; south, 17, 25-6, 27-8, 32, 35, 39, 40, 59, 64; west, 21
Constantinople, 14, 15, 106
Copper, 71, 72, 78

203

CRETE

Cotton, 152
Crusade, Fourth, 98
Cypress, 54
Cyrene, 93

Daskaloyanni, 124
Deforestation, 28, 49, 145
Development Plan, Cretan, 64, 138–9, 143
Dhia, 30, 195
Dhikti, Mt, 30, 35, 36
Donkeys, 11, 53, 60–1
Dorians, 89–91
Dress, traditional, 11, 164

Earthquakes, 76, 83, 170, 173, 174, 186
Eastern Roman Empire, 94–9
Education, 193–4
Egypt, 68, 72, 74, 79, 125–8, 178
Elounda, 17, 38, 59
Enosis, see Union with Greece
Eteocretans, 85
Evans, Sir Arthur, 67, 68, 72, 79–86 *passim*

Faïence, 78
Farms, 147–9
Flowers, 54, 69
Flying-boat service, 17
Fodder crops, 53
Food, 50, 154–6, 188
Fourni, 37, 59
Fruit trees, 48, 54, 151, 152, 155

Garrigue, 48, 49
Gavdhos, 196–7
Geology, 19–40 *passim*
Gergeri, 29, 32
Geropotamos, R., 32
Goats, 49, 54–5, 147, 153–4
Gold, 78

Gonia, 21
Gortys, 31, 93, 95, 96
Gortys, Laws of, 89, 90–1
Gournia, 74
Grabousa, 116, 123, 125, 195
Grandes Is, 39, 197
Grapes, *see* Sultanas, Table-grapes and Wine-grapes
Greece, 81–2, 92, 94, 124–5
Greek language, 9–10, 82–3
Greenhouses, 48, 152

Halepa, Pact of, 131–2
Hieroglyphic scripts, 78–9
Hornet pendant, 78
Hospitals, 194
Hotels, 141, 184, 187, 188–9
Housing, rural, 145; urban, 171, 178, 180
Hutchinson, R. W., 68, 74, 85

Idha, Mt (Psiloritis), 20, 28–9, 43, 64, 105, 108, 129
Ierapetra, 38–9, 48, 58, 59, 66, 93, 108, 114, 132, 165
Industry, 156–64, 168, 172, 178, 181
Iraklion, 50, 60–6 *passim*, 94–6, 99, 101, 112–13, 118–23, 132, 135, 150, 165, 168–77, 185, 188, 189, 191, 194; airport, 17–18, 141; climate, 41–2; port, 15, 16, 31, 102, 124, 141, 162
Iron, 61
Irrigation, 32, 36, 40, 45, 61, 75, 151, 152, 186–7
Iuktas, Mt, 30
Ivory, 72

Kakodikianos, R., 21
Kallergai family, 109–11, 113, 114
Kapsas, 39

INDEX

Kastelli Kissamou, 22, 62, 63, 166
Kastelli Pedhiadhos, 30
Kavousi, 62, 64
Khania, 22, 48, 60–6 *passim*, 93, 101, 110, 114, 115, 118, 123, 125, 132, 137, 151, 160, 165, 177–81, 188, 191, 194; airport, 17, 22; port, 14–16, 22, 61, 102
Kharakas, 32
Khersonisos, 31, 48
Khora Sphakion, 25, 26, 27, 129
Khrysolakkos, 78
Khrysoskalitissa, Monastery, 21
Knossos, 59, 62, 67–89 *passim*, 92, 93, 171, 177
Kokkinos Pirgos, 32
Kolymbari, 57, 61
Kounavi, 32
Kournas, Lake, 23
Krakatau, 84
Kritsa, 165–7
Kythera, 14, 16

Lassithi, 35–7, 45, 65–7 *passim*, 101, 114, 137, 194
Lassithi Mts, 30, 35–8
Lato, 184–5
Law, 90–1, 103, 191–2; *see also* Gortys, Laws of
Lefka Ori (White Mts), 20, 22, 23, 24–6, 54, 133
Leper colony, 185
Libya, 72, 74, 75
Limnes, 37
Linear, A, 80, 81
Linear B, 81–3, 86
Lion of St Mark, 11, 172
Litton Inc, 141–3
Loutra, 25–6

Macedonia, 92, 98
Maleme airfield, 17, 137

Malevisi, 100
Mallia, 31, 48, 62, 72, 75–6, 78, 80, 85
Maquis, 47, 49–50
Marinatos, S., 83–4
Marketing, 61, 64
Matala, 35
Megaron, 86
Mercenaries, Cretan, 89
Mesopotamia, 68, 74
Messara Plain, 27, 29, 31–2, 48, 59, 71, 72, 74, 76, 105, 142, 151, 152
Milatos, 31, 35, 37, 85
Mills, wind and water, 35, 36, 37, 58, 90, 113, 160–2
Minoans, 28, 31, 39, 68–85, 154–5, 187
Mires, 31, 59, 165, 166
Mithridates, 92
Mokhlos, 21, 40, 72, 79, 196
Monasteries, 21, 29, 36, 37, 40, 129–30, 187
Monofatsi, 100
Morosini, 118–20, 173
Motor vehicles, 63, 65, 168
Mountains, 12, 19–40 *passim*, 45, 53–5, 61, 62, 64, 153
Mournies, 127–8, 166
Mules, 53, 59, 60–1, 63
Myceneans, 81, 82–3, 85–9
Mylopotamos, R., 24

NATO base, 22
Neapolis, 35, 37, 50, 64, 66, 166, 167, 184
Neolithic age, 67–8, 71, 76
Nerokouros, 166
Nidha, plain, 28–9, 45

Obsidian, 67, 72
Olives, 22, 29, 48, 50, 105, 151; oil, 61, 105, 126, 148, 149, 155, 160

Omalos, 24–5, 45, 60, 129

Pakhia Ammos, 38, 56–7, 62
Pakhnes, 24
Palaeokhora, 21, 25, 108
Palaeolithic age, 67
Palaikastro, 39, 58, 74, 187
Palm trees, 40, 48
Pantelis, R., 40, 186
Parking restrictions, 66
Pasture, 48, 49, 54–5, 147, 153–4
Peanuts, 23
Pedhiadha, 30, 100, 114
Pendlebury, J. D. S., 58–9, 60, 67, 72, 74
Perama, 24
Peza, 32
Phaistos, 31, 59, 72, 75–6, 80, 85
Phaistos disk, 80–1
Phalasarna, 21
Phodele, 24
Piraeus, 13, 15, 16, 56
Pirates, 94, 99, 107, 115, 182, 186
Police, tourist and other, 189, 191–2
Poljes, 24, 26, 37, 40
Population, 74–5, 89, 93, 135, 146–7, 165–7
Postal services, 189–90
Pottery, 67–74 *passim*, 83
Pseira, 74, 196
Psiloritis, *see* Idha, Mt
Psychro, 36
Public services, 145, 147, 161
Pumice, 84–5

Railway, lack of, 56
Rainfall, 42–5 *passim*
Raulin, V., 14–15, 60, 63
Reafforestation, 49
Religion, 96, 104, 112, 123–6 *passim*, 179, 190
Rendzina, 30, 54

Restaurants, 102–3, 162, 168, 188
Rethymnon, 23, 26–8, 48, 62, 64, 65, 66, 101, 116, 118, 165, 181–3, 188, 191, 194; port, 15, 16, 23, 124
Revolts, 107–17, 124–5, 128–32
Rhodhopou, 22
Rivers, 24, 25, 28, 32, 40
Roads, early, 58–61, 102, 124, 171; modern, 27, 32, 36, 37, 61–6, 181, 182, 186
Road signs, 66
Rogdhia, 19, 24, 30, 31
Romans, 35, 36, 92–4

St George of Selinari, Monastery, 37
St Paul, 35
Salterns, 38
Samaria gorge, 25, 147
Santorini, *see* Thira
Sea routes, early, 13–16; modern, 16–17, 56, 181
Sealstones, 72, 78–9
Selinari gorge, 35, 37, 62, 64
Selinon, 20–1, 57–8, 100, 108
Sheep, 49, 54–5, 63, 138, 147, 153–4
Shipping, 38, 56–8, 77, 105, 129–30, 168, 181, 182
Shipsheds, 172, 178
Shops, 145–6, 162, 173, 180
Shrubs, 47, 48, 49
Silk, 106, 152
Sitia, 16, 40, 45, 53, 56, 59, 66, 101, 114, 115, 132, 137, 160, 165, 185, 186–7, 188
Snake goddess, 78
Snow, 42, 45
Soapstone, *see* Steatite
Social organisation, 86–9, 91, 96, 100–1, 104
Soils, 22, 25–30 *passim*, 40, 45, 53, 54

Soudha, 16, 17, 22, 62, 108, 115, 116, 123, 137, 162, 181, 195
Soumadha, 50
Sphakia, 85, 95, 108, 110, 114, 116, 123, 137
Sphakia gorge, 26
Spinalonga, 38, 59, 108, 116, 123, 132, 185, 195–6
Spratt, Capt T. A. B., 59, 184
Stavrochori, 61
Steatite, 72, 78, 79
Stirrup jars, 83
Stone Age, 67–8, 71
Sub-alpine zone, 45, 54–5
Sugar, 106
Sultanas, 48, 50, 53, 150, 159–60, 172, 187
Swallow-holes, 25, 29, 35–6
Syria, 72, 74

Table-grapes, 48, 50, 53, 150, 187
Tavronitis, R., 61
Taxis, 56, 63
Telephones, 190
Terracing, 28, 53, 147
Textiles, 162
Therissos, 133
Thira, 16, 56, 83–5
Timios Stavros, 28
Titos, St, 95, 96, 112, 174, 190
Tombs, 72
Toplou, Monastery, 40, 187
Towns, 74–5, 165–87
Tractors, single-axle, 65
Trade, 72, 105–6, 150, 152, 162, 181, 185
Traffic lights, 174
Transport, early, 59–61, 75 modern, 65–6, 148, 168, 182
Trees, 48–50 *passim*, 53–4, 152; *see also* Fruit trees

Trevor-Battye, A. B. R., 57–8, 60, 61
Turks, 59, 114–35, 152, 174, 179, 180, 182–6 *passim*, 189
Tylissos, 30, 86
Tymbaki, 32, 165, 166
Tzermiades, 36

Union with Greece, 12, 113, 128–9, 132, 134–5

Vaï, 39, 40, 48, 187
Vasiliki, 72
Vegetables, 39, 48, 148, 151, 152, 155, 187
Vegetation, 45–55
Venetians, 14, 38, 98–117, 173–80, 182–3, 185, 186
Venezelos, E., 133–6
Villages, 144–7, 165
Vines, 26, 29, 48, 50, 53, 105, 146, 148, 149–51, 155
Volakias, 24
Vrondisi, Monastery, 29

White Mts, *see* Lefka Ori
Windpumps, 36
Wine, 105–6, 126, 149–50, 159
Wine-grapes, 40, 50, 53, 105, 149–50
World War I, 61, 135
World War II, 38, 63, 136–7, 170, 178

Xiloskalo, 25

Zakros, 39, 58, 72, 86, 187
Zaros, 29, 32, 166
Zeus, 36, 64, 67
Ziros, 40